THE AUGUSTAN REPRINT

DONAIDES

JOHN KER

(1725)

AND

A POEM

In Imitation of

DONAIDES

[DAVID MALLOCH]

(*1725*)

Introduction by
IRMA S. LUSTIG
and a translation by
BARROWS DUNHAM

PUBLICATION NUMBER *188*

WILLIAM ANDREWS CLARK MEMORIAL LIBRARY

UNIVERSITY OF CALIFORNIA, LOS ANGELES

1978

INTRODUCTION

The occasional poems reprinted here as they were first issued, in tandem, are as different in style and method as they are in length, though one is an "imitation" of the other. John Ker's *Donaides* is an allegorical tribute in Latin verse to James Fraser, Licenser of the Press in the reign of King James II, the first Secretary of Chelsea Hospital, and an alumnus and benefactor of King's College, Aberdeen.[1] Fraser's gifts of books and funds at a crucial time enabled the college to expand the library holdings and to replace the library itself, the jewel house, and the dormitories on the south side of the quadrangle. The university expressed its gratitude by conferring on Fraser the degree J.U.D. (*Juris Utriusque Doctor*, Doctor of Civil and Canon Law), 29 March 1725.[2] Ker, Professor of Greek, read *Donaides* at the ceremony, and Thomas Ruddiman published it for the university late the same year. So far as I know *Donaides* is now reprinted for the first time, though it affords a close view of the Scottish Reformation, and is a basic source of information—sometimes the only source—about the early years of King's College.

Donaides was advertised as "Just now published" in the *Caledonian Mercury* (also printed by Ruddiman) for 23 November 1725, "to which is annexed," it was added, "an English poem, in Imitation of the Latin, by David Malloch, A.M.[3] The Whole, consisting of Four Sheets, is to be sold . . . in Edinburgh; and . . . in Aberdeen" (No. 882, p. 5642). This notice explains why the sixty-six lines of couplets by Malloch were printed on three sides of a quarto half-sheet, and though numbered independently, lack title page, imprint, and date. The reader will observe that the rectangular device above the title also ornaments the first page of *Donaides*. Yale's copy of the imitation is yoked with *Donaides* in an old binding, and the National Library of Scotland and the libraries of the universities of Aberdeen and Edinburgh also report that the poems are bound together in their holdings.[4] It is clear from young Malloch's published letters to Ker, his mentor, and probably his teacher,[5] that Ker had commissioned the English rendering for joint publication with his Latin original.[6]

I have been at pains to discover and summarize the facts of publication because the letters "A. M." are appended to Malloch's name, though he had no degree in 1725. He had attended the University of Edinburgh, but he had never taken a degree, as Malloch himself wrote to Ker 29 December 1725. He added at once that "when your Society bestows that honour upon me, I will return them my thanks in a letter addressed to the whole body" (ii [September 1793], 171). Malloch had a printed copy of his poem at hand when he wrote that statement, for in the very letter which contains it he made caustic observations on his own and the printer's blunders.

The degree he obviously anticipated was awarded 11 January 1726, when "the Masters having formerly seen and approven an English Poem written by Mr. David Malloch, Tutor to the Duke of Montrose's sons, in imitation of the *Donaides*, and having ordered the same to be published therewith, they, as a mark of their esteem and respect for the said Mr. Malloch, and being sufficiently satisfied of his good Letters and bright qualifications otherways, unanimously agreed that a Diploma shall be sent to him conferring on him the Degree of Mr. of Arts in this University."[7] It seems reasonable to conclude that the administrators of the university authorized Ruddiman to append the degree to Malloch's name when the imitation went to press in November 1725.

Professor Ker and David Malloch differed as much in their critical commitments as they did in age and era. Ker was a mature humanist and academic when Latin was the pride of Scottish intellectual life. He was made Professor of Humanity (Latin) at the University of Edinburgh in 1734, and he was a member of the distinguished society which Thomas Ruddiman and other learned men founded at Edinburgh in 1718 "for improving each other in classical lore."[8] *Donaides* is a poem of noble design, a candid and methodical history of the University of Aberdeen composed in 301 Latin hexameters introduced by six elegiac couplets. The narrative advances chronologically, in a pattern of cycles, from the founding of King's College in 1494 by William Elphinstone, Bishop of Aberdeen, through glory (early, and twice renewed), corruption, and political struggle, to a moving climax of Fraser's munificence and the praises of a grateful community.

Ker adopted the conventions as well as the language of the ancients, a Miltonic framework, more pagan than Christian, of classical names, allusions, and rhetorical devices. The *Donaides* of the title makes punning allusion to the Danaides, the fifty daughters of Danaus in the well-known myth,[9] but the name means in fact the daughters of Dona, the river Don, at the mouth of which the city of Aberdeen is situated. (Aberdeen indeed *means* "mouth of the Don,"[10] as Ker reminded the reader when he noted at the end of his poem *"Scribebam ad ostia Donæ in vicinia Coll. Regii Aberdonen."*) As Professor Dunham and I explain in detail in note 1 to the translation, the *Donaides*, the Aberdonian Muses who sing the hymn of thanksgiving, represent allegorically all the noble academic aspects of King's College, past and present. That identification is justified grammatically, for the Greek patronymic suffix is of common gender.

That Ker intended a dual translation is indicated by a second memorial exercise. When Fraser died in May 1731, aged 86, bequeathing the college furniture and considerable funds for salaries and bursaries, Ker wrote a funeral oration and elegy which was also read at the College and published the next year. The title of that poem is *Frasereides.*[11]

Ker could not have been surprised by the brief and generalized imitation he got from Malloch. They had corresponded at least from 1720, when at Ker's recommendation Malloch was acting as tutor to the four sons of Home of Dreghorn. Malloch solicited Ker's advice on the programs he outlined for his pupils, his own education, and the poems he was writing (four of them were published in the *Edinburgh Miscellany*, 1720.[12]) But from the outset Malloch's own views were precise and decided, and his letters a delicate balance of deference and assurance. As early as 1720 Ker asked him to translate his "Congratulatory Poem" from the Latin. Malloch declared his independence of academic imitations, and wrote of his finished work that he had generally "steered a middle course" between paraphrase and literal translation, careful, however, to render the sense "perfect and unmaimed." Paraphrase was the way to elegance, he explained (amidst many apologies), because there is such a "weight and energy" in the Latin phrases. And he had omitted proper names "industriously," because they are sounding and harmonious in Latin, but so flat in a translation that they give "a kind of littleness to the verse, by being always in the mouth of the vulgar" (i [January 1793], 5).

These principles of generalization, creative fidelity, and euphony are reiterated in Malloch's letters to Ker as late as 1727, and guide his hand in the imitation of *Donaides*. Too busy (was he really?) to make a literal translation of the copy of *Donaides* he received in June 1725, he announced himself resolved to raise a shorter work on Ker's foundation. The poem would turn on the ruinous condition of the University and on Ker's bounty, and end with a general encomium on the faculty, with "particular mention of its most deserving member and my best Friend." Malloch heartily approved of allegory, and he praised Ker for calling to the assistance of a poem necessarily didactic "those imaginary beings that poetry uses to support the dignity of the facts she recites." Without apology, however, he criticized the lists of Latinized Scots names in *Donaides* ("Poetry is always addressing itself to the fancy; and no numbers please the fancy that offend the ear.") He admired the graceful incorporation of passages from Ovid and Virgil, but will not "some readers" tax Ker with plagiarism, he asked, for transcribing without alteration whole lines such as the thirteen he now cited (ii [September 1793], 196 [169]-170)?

Malloch worked hastily, and the imitation was finished by September. It is almost one fifth the length of its model, and historically uninformative, sometimes even misleading, because Malloch telescoped events, and strove for elevation by substituting italicized abstractions and moralizing generalities for fact. Of all the significant actors only Bishop Elphinstone and Principal Gordon are named. The poem does "rise," as Professor Dunham claims with much better reason for *Donaides*, but it is easy to discover its numerous flaws as one stutters over the alliteration. Some allowance must be made for Malloch, however.

His method was deliberate, as we have seen, and based on principles adopted early but thoughtfully. John Ramsay of Ochtertyre remarked that in the earlier part of the eighteenth century nothing could induce young Scots to emulate the men writing poetry in Latin, because "they could only expect to attain to mediocrity," and in editing Ramsay's manuscript Alexander Allardyce noted that Ker was at least the most voluminous writer of Latin verse in his time, if not the best. "By writing in English [Ramsay concludes], which few of them could speak with elegance and propriety, was opened a more ready road to fame and excellence."[13] Malloch's letters to Ker show that even as a young man he was ambitious and intellectually confident. He was skillful enough in Latin to translate the poetry of a distinguished professor of the classics, but in taking up Ker's commissions he had to compete with his patron. He was at a disadvantage, moreover, because he lacked the parallel but distant circumstances essential to a true imitation. By adopting a different mode Malloch impressed the reader with his originality and his modernity.

Ker was generous in advancing his protégé, but slow to grant him as much independence as Malloch claimed. He took the liberty of altering Malloch's verses, despite insistent and well-reasoned protests. Robert Anderson's reprintings of what he identified as the original manuscript copy of the *Imitation* show that Malloch first wrote at lines 23-24,

> Zeal, pious to a crime, reform'd the age,
> And Gothic purity, and priestly rage.[14]

Ker objected that the lines could be interpreted as a satire on the Reformation in general. Malloch replied that they were intended to satirize some particular persons "whose well-meaning but intemperate zeal betrayed them into a ridiculous fury against stone and timber." He opposed Ker's intended replacement,

> When *Sacred Structures* fell by *popular Rage*,
> Old *Gothick* Piles, not modish for the Age.

The first line, he wrote, is "harsh and unharmonious," and the second flat and unmeaning. ("Did the Reformers then pull down these edifices because they were unfashionable?") He implored Ker to emend the whole passage as Malloch now gave it in his letter,[15] and he preferred that the entire poem be suppressed rather than printed without the change (ii [July 1793], 2-3).

Ker disregarded Malloch's wishes, as the facsimile shows. In his anguish Malloch cursed the whole paragraph where he had inveighed against Avarice and Zeal and violated his own common sense in order to please people who did not have enough to discover his blunder. The poem was "entire, and tolerable" without lines 19 to 26, he wrote to Ker 29 December 1725 (ii [September 1793], 171), and he deleted them from the text printed in *Poems on Several Occasions*, 1743.[16] The paragraph must already have been cancelled (and the internal punctuation of 1. 55 restored) in the corrected copy of the panegyric, now lost, which Malloch had printed at London early in 1726 (ii [August 1793], [89]). It may not have been until 1743, however, that Malloch redirected the slurs in 11. 3-4 from peers to bishops, and exalted the years

> Ere mitred Pride, which arts alone had rais'd,
> Those very arts, in others, saw, unprais'd.

Ker was sufficiently pleased with Malloch's *Imitation* not only to have it printed with *Donaides* in 1725, but also to send Malloch before the year was out another of his poems for translation. Malloch himself took satisfaction in some features of his imitation: the beauty of his "short allegories," like Charity's prophetic speech to Learning, and the "purely poetical" images he recommended to Ker's notice, "Time shaking your arches, and mouldering your piles; as also Ruin, with his imaginary companion Silence." He judged the lines which memorialize Fraser's gift of books "perhaps the best in the whole poem" (ii [July 1793], i). Except for a few minor verbal changes, these favorite lines and phrases remained untouched in Malloch's subsequent revisions of the *Imitation*.

Malloch remade his poem as he remade himself (to paraphrase a later and greater poet), and in the 1759 edition of his *Works* the remnant of political strife was transferred to powerless academics. "Fair Charity," who previously had commanded an end to Faction and Discord, now asked that "low self-love and pedant-discord cease." Two lines were added to the poem, and it was rephrased freely from line fourteen to the end.[17] This bland third version of the *Imitation* became the standard text, and was reprinted in the numerous multi-volume collections of poetry of the eighteenth and early nineteenth centuries. Cut free from its model in 1743, the *Imitation* was retitled "Verses Occasioned by Dr. Fraser's Rebuilding Part of the University of Aberdeen," the name it bore thereafter.

By 1817 Alexander Bower, historian of the University of Edinburgh, could find no copy of *Donaides* in the city's public libraries, although it was represented in the catalogues.[18] The *Imitation* sank quietly from sight after 1822. Although Boswell immortalized both poems of 1725 in the *Life of Johnson*, the *Imitation* published with *Donaides* is here reprinted for the first time. Whatever literary merits the poems are judged to possess, they have great interest as paradigms of cultural change and the struggle of the generations.[19]

Irma S. Lustig
Yale University

NOTES TO THE INTRODUCTION

1. Robert Sangster Rait, *The Universities of Aberdeen* (Aberdeen, 1895), pp. 193, 237, 242; R. B. Litchfield, *Notes and Queries*, 9th Series, iii (22 April 1899), 301-302.

2. Peter John Anderson, *Roll of Alumni in Arts of the University and King's College of Aberdeen, 1596-1860* (Aberdeen, 1900), p. 23.

3. Later Mallet, the versifier ("William and Margaret") and dramatist notorious as the disciple of Pope who at the service of Lord Bolingbroke defamed him posthumously; secretary to the factious Prince of Wales, and sinecurist to Lord Bute. Johnson had pilloried Mallet in the abridged edition (1756) of the *Dictionary* for changing his name after he had settled in England: *Alias:* "A Latin word, signifying otherwise; as, Mallet *alias* Malloch; that is, *otherwise* Malloch."

4. The copies at the British Library are bound and shelved separately, but they otherwise conform to the description above of the other printed poems.

5. Malloch was born around 1702 (some biographers say 1705) near Crieff, Perthshire, where Ker was master of the parish school until 1710. Malloch appears to have been janitor of the high school in Edinburgh in 1717, when Ker, the highly esteemed Principal, left to take up his appointment at King's College. (Robert Anderson, ed., *A Complete Edition of the Poets of Great Britain*, 13 vols. [London, 1794], ix. [669]; Frederick Dinsdale, ed., *Mallet's Ballads and Songs* [London, 1857], pp. 12, 17-19; H. W. Starr, "Notes on David Mallet," *Notes and Queries*, clxxviii [20 April 1940], 277-278.)

6. Eighteen letters which Mallet wrote to Ker between 5 October 1720 and 31 July 1727 were printed monthly in the *Edinburgh Magazine*, New Series, edited by Robert Anderson, January through November 1793. The sequence was reprinted with all its errors of dating and order in the *European Magazine*, May through November 1793 and January and February 1794. The dates which I assign to the letters in this introduction are explained in my article, "David Malloch's Published Letters to John Ker Redated," *The Papers of the Bibliographical Society of America* 72:2 (1978). The citations of the letters are to the *Edinburgh Magazine*; they will be found within parentheses in the text of the introduction.

7. *Roll of Alumni*, Appendix A, p. [193].

8. Alexander Bower, *The History of the University of Edinburgh*, 3 vols. (Edinburgh, 1817), ii. 296–297; George Chalmers, *The Life of Thomas Ruddiman* (London, 1794), pp. 83-84.

9. Samuel Johnson was clearly making this analogy when he asked James Boswell to inquire of Lord Hailes, who had sent him a copy of Malloch's *Imitation*, "WHO was Donaus of whom Donaides was the son." (*Private Papers of James Boswell from Malahide Castle In the Collection of Lt-Colonel Ralph Heyward Isham*, 18 vols. [Mt. Vernon, New York, 1928-34], 15 (1932), 208 [30 April 1783].) Boswell asked Johnson for the copy of the *Imitation*, which he would keep as a "curiosity," and indeed, it is now in the Dyce Collection

at the Victoria and Albert Museum. But Boswell did not report the query when he translated the conversation about Malloch's poem to the *Life of Johnson*. For a detailed discussion of the matter, see Irma S. Lustig, "'Donaus,' *Donaides*, and David Malloch: A Reply to Dr. Johnson," *Modern Philology* 76:1 (August 1978).

10. Margaret Gelling et al., *The Names of Towns and Cities in Britain* (London, 1970), pp. 35-36. The town was called *Aberdon* in the twelfth century, and its inhabitants are still called *Aberdonians*.

11. Rait, *The Universities of Aberdeen*, p. 194.

12. R. C. Boys, "Malloch and the *Edinburgh Miscellany*," *Modern Language Notes*, liv (1939), 468–469.

13. *Scotland and Scotsmen in the Eighteenth Century*, 2 vols. (Edinburgh, 1888), i. 38 and n. 1.

14. *Edinburgh Magazine*, ii (November 1793), 341-342; *A Complete Edition of the Poets of Great Britain*, ix. 682-683.

15.   But now, the years, revolving, backward ran;
                And a dark series of worse time began.
                Vile Avarice, a cruel spoiler rose,
                And Fraud, and Rapine, all-destroying foes!
                With these the giddy vulgar fir'd to rage;
                While pious Zeal reform'd an erring age;
                Then the fair sister-arts began to pine,
                Then Learning saw his falling state decline.
                Without assaulted, and within betray'd;
                And every Muse's portion was unpaid!

16. (London, 1943), p. [201].

17. *The Works of David Malloch Esq.*, 3 vols. (London, 1759), i. [35].

18. *History of the University of Edinburgh*, i. 299.

19. It gives me pleasure to acknowledge the invaluable assistance of Professor Frederick A. Pottle, Chairman of the Editorial Committee of the Yale Editions of the Private Papers of James Boswell, and the generous support of the Research and Editing Programs of the National Endowment for the Humanities. I acknowledge as well the satisfaction of joint publication with Professor Dunham, my earliest and most influential mentor and my greatly valued friend.

BIBLIOGRAPHICAL NOTE

Donaides (1725) and "Poem in Imitation of *Donaides*" (1725) are reproduced from the copies bound together (Shelf Mark: Gr 17/14.) in the Beinecke Rare Book and Manuscript Library, Yale University. A typical type-page (p. 5) of *Donaides* measures 176 x 97 mm; of "Imitation" (p. 3) 182 x 116 mm.

DONAIDES:
SIVE

Musarum Aberdonensium

De eximia

JACOBI FRASERII, J.U.D.

In Academiam Regiam *Aberdonensem* munificentia, Carmen Eucharisticum.

Notis illustratum, quibus strictim perscribitur Historia Universitatis & Collegii Regii ABERDONENSIS, *à primævâ ipsius Institutione, ad nostra usque tempora perpetuâ serie.*

Auctore JOANNE KER, Græcarum Literarum Professore in Academiâ Regiâ ABERDONENSI.

EDINBURGI, in ædibus THO. RUDDIMANNI, 1725.

DONAIDES:

Sive Muſarum ABERDONENSIUM, de eximia *Jacobi Fraſerii*, J. U. D. in Academiam Regiam A-
BERDONENSEM munificentia, Carmen Euchari-
ſticum.

A*Ccipe,* FRASERI, *generoſe ac inclyte factis,*
    Quæ tibi Donaïdes *munera parva ferunt ;*
    Munera parva quidem, nec quæ tua maxima dona
    Æquent : aſt inopes nos humileſque decent.
Te penes argentum eſt, auri & tibi copia flavi ;
    Noſque beas dando, te ſimul ipſe beas :
Noſque damus quæ fert hortus munuſcula noſter,
    Purpureos flores, lilia miſta roſis.

IA alacres hilareſque Virum cantemus, amœnos
    Qui nobis reddit lucos & tecta ſuperba.
     Atria Muſarum ſtudiis ſacrata manebant
    Exornata diu, bene ſarta & tecta, perennes
5 Quas *Elphinſtonius*, pietate inſignis   *in oris*
His Ædes conſtituit nobis, ſedemque locavit

Regali

Regali imperio, Regis de nomine dictam :
Multa ubi certatim per quædam sæcla juventus:
Exercere artes, studia & celebrare frequenti
10 Agmine consuevit, lætasque agitare choreas.
    PHOEBO olim hâc unâ sedes non gratior ulla,
Nec quâ formosus se plus jactaret Apollo :
Huc, latices linquens sacros, Permessidas undas,
Et juga Parnassi, pulcherrimæ ad ostia *Donæ*
15 Nos secum avectas subduxit, jussa secutus
Ipsa Jovis summi. Tunc talia fatus, " Arenâ
  " Optatâ fruimur, quas celsas cernitis arces
  " Sunt *Elphinstonii*, sublimibus alta columnis
  " Regia, quam vobis statuit, propriamque dicavit.
20 " Huc nos fata vocant, has nunc migremus in ædes ;
  " Hæc jam nostra domus, nostra hæc & flumina, fontes;
  " Hi nostri, hi colles aprici & cuncta vireta.
    Nec mora, lætantes properamus tendere gressus,
Patre Deo monstrante viam, sacrata subimus
25 Mœnia, nosque novas arces & Dædala tecta
Suspicere usque juvat ; sedesque habitare beatas
Contigit, & placidâ compostas pace manere.
    Jamque tuas linquunt, formosa *Lutetia*, turres.
Pierides ; celeres formosæ ad flumina *Donæ*
30 Corripiunt gressus, & avent sibi ponere sedem.
Hector adest ! agmen ducens celeberrimus ille
Boetius noster, comes *Haius* fidus Achates :
Florent tunc Musæ, fulgent & nomina docta.
Prisca *Caledoniæ* sic *Gallia* dona rependit,
35 Carolus & Magnus SCOTO sua munera reddit.
    Post *Elphinstonium*, *Dunbari* & sacra *Stuarti*
Insula nos texit ; multosque peregimus annos
Felices ; pleno manabat copia cornu.
Flumina jam lactis, jam flumina nectaris ibant ;
40 Flavaque de viridi stillabant ilice mella :
Liber & alma Ceres donabant munera sponte.

Frondebant sylvæ, florebant arva colonis.
Tecta renidebant, lychni laquearibus aurefs
Pendebant, choreas lætas plaudente coronâ.

45   DETERIOR posthac ætas, volventibus annis,
Orta est, *Gordonio* rerum potiente facrarum.
Protinus erupit venæ pejoris in ævum
Omne nefas : fugère pudor, verumque fidefque,
In quorum fubiére locum fraudefque dolique,
50 Infidiæque & vis, & amor fceleratus habendi.
Non *Elphinftonii* fimilis *Gordonius*, omnes,
Turpiter at cenfus fundofque abfumit avitos,
Quæque *Elphinftonius* facrârat dona *Minervæ*.
Te tamen hîc laudes & honos, *Leslæe*, manebit.

55   NEVE infons (fas vera loqui quæ vidimus ipfæ)
Heu! pia gens nimium, ftudio dùm concita cæco,
Sævit in auguftas ædes & Palladis arces,
Dumque ftudet plumbum facrato avellere Templo :
Horrendum fic aufa nefas (quis talia fando
60 Temperet à lachrymis!) patrare, aufoque potita
Effet, magnanimus ni fortiter obvius iffet
Andreades, noftri vindex noftrique facelli.
Noftra quoque Archiva & fervata, ereptaque morti,
Regales chartas, multa & diplomata monftrant.

65   NEC tamen & nobis finis fuit ille malorum :
Infontes patriâ germanas pellere certant.
Exiliumque *Themis* patitur, Medicina fugatur,
Refque fuas juffus fibi *Juftinianus* habere,
Gregoriufque pater decreta auferre jubetur ;
70 *Hippocratefque* fenex pulfus, fimul atque *Galenus* ;
Orpheus & clarus cithârâ fidibufque canoris
Flectere feu fuperos dirum aut Acheronta movere,
Non movet hos ; ac ad delphinas miffus *Arion*.
Sic laniata comas, artus laniata jacebat
75 *Alma* dolens *Mater* ; mœrentia limina fervant,
Horrendum! malefuada Fames & turpis Egeftas.

RES-

RESPICIUNT tandem miseras pia numina Musas:
Qui Jovis imperio *Scotis* sua jura ministrat,
Largus opum nobis *Jacobus* nomine Sextus
80 De locupletę penu fundit sua munera, terris
Nos variis donans, variis proventibus augens.
Hîc, *Metelane*, tuum nomen super astra feremus,
Hîcque tuum, *Arbuthnote*, tuum &, divine *Stuarte*.

  NEC tamen hisce frui licuit per nomina fœda,
85 *Harpyias* avidas : quæ rapta cibaria nobis
Unguibus, ab ! uncis lacerabant omnia diræ.
Donec *Patricius* clarus *Forbesius* ille,
Corsius, à fundis nomen sortitus avitis,
Unus qui nobis collapsam restituit rem,
90 Omnibus exhaustas prope cladibus, omnium egenas
Nos miseras, humiles, penitus penitusque jacentes
Erexit ; calidoque sinu complexus hic *Almam*
Effœtam Matrem multâ sobolescere fecit
Prole novâ, & viridis revirescere flore juventæ.
95 Is census raptos & fundos reddit avitos ;
Harpyias dare terga fugæ trepidantia cogit.
Hoc duce, prisca *Themis* redit, & sua jura ministrat ;
Cous & ipse redux turbâ stipatus ovanti ;
Orpheus hinc psallit, cantat vocalis *Arion*.
100 Jamque iterum nobis priscum renovatur in aurum
Ætas ; Pierides jam florea rura pererrant,
Impediuntque comas sertis Pæana canentes.

  PATRICIO extincto, dolor eheu ! quantus obortus ?
Orba parente suo mœrens Academia plorat ;
105 Plorat & amissum pallens Ecclesia Patrem ;
Regia nec tanti fuit exsors ipsa doloris ;
Luget & hunc lachrymis oculos suffusa nitentes
Pallas operta caput, deflevit & ultima *Thule* :
Tueda pater raucis gemit hunc ululatibus ; ingens
110 Fluctibus undisonis plangit sua brachia ripis
Glotta fremens; rapidoque *Taus* devectus ab alto

                                             Vertice

Vertice *Grampiaco* contorquet vortice lymphas ;
Dona retro properat, verfifque relabitur undis
In juga *Grampigenûm* ; *Dea* fævos fertur in æstus
115 *Oceani*, fremitu volvens ad fidera fluctus.
Nos, uti par, vario confperfum flore rofarum
Huic facimus tumulum, carmenque infcribimus illi.

    SED non occubuit totus *Forbefius* ingens ;
Verùm orta ex aureô hoc funt lumina fidere clara,
120 Quæ ftupuit Tellus gelido fubjecta Trioni
Per multos annos : linquis, Pater optime, natum
Te dignum, cujus nomen per fæcla vigebit,
Si pietatis honos, doctrinæ aut gratia quævis.

    CAROLUS hinc primus, quos infula facra *Donenfis*
125 Sacratos habuit cenfus, cernente Senatu,
Ablatos nullam voluit temerare profanam
Dextram, fed nobis fanctis noftroque Lycæo
Sacravit totos, Mufas miferatus egenas ;
(Unde novas ftudio præclaras furgere magno
130 Fecimus, inque altum pulchras ereximus arces.)
Quos & reddidimus, folio cum natus avito
Redditur atque Pàtris, tulimus nec præmia magna.

    NEC pofthac aliquo fuperi nos munere donant,
Dum nos refpexit miferas *Aurantius heros*,
135 Palladis egregius cultor bellique togæque ;
Anna Pia & nofmet refpexit lumine læto.
Quæ dedit *Anna*, bonus renovavit *Georgius* Almæ
Matri, ne premeret nos turpis inedia triftes.

    PRIVATI quidam *Matrem* tunc temporis *Almam*
140 Afficiunt donis, quos omnes longa referre
Hîc mora : fed te non hîc fas, *Buchane*, filere ;
Aulaï in medio pateris libemus & auro
Jure tibi, cujus juffu noftra Aula novata eft.

    HIC memorare Viros par eft qui Bibliothecam
145 Ditârunt libris ; capit aft non pagina noftra :
Teque tuumque tamen natum, *Scugalle*, tacere

Non fas : nec veſtrum nomen, *Gardene*, *Fraſeri*,
Nec vos, *Strachane*, hîc, *Rhæde*, aut, *Burnete*, ſilebo.
   H I C quoque, qui Burſas donârunt laudibus æquis,
150 Fas celebrare Viros, ni nos mora longa teneret.
   Agmen *Burnetus* ducit, comitesque ſequuntur
Wattus, *Ogilvæus*, *Melvillus*, *Parkus*, *Adamus*,
Fullartonæus, *Watſonus*, *Bracconiana*,
Et *Falconerus*, poſtremus denique *Greggus*.
155 Hæ jam felices animæ, pia nomina, lætos
Devenêre locos hilares, & amœna vireta
Fortunatorum nemorum ſedeſque beatas.
   N E C tamen interea res ſalva eſt noſtra, minantur
Tecta *Elphinſtonii* caſum triſteſque ruinas :
160 Jam fœdi viſu cineres & rudera multa ;
Jamque ſolo æquata, ah ! *Dunbaria* tecta jacebant :
Jamque iterum *Harpyiæ*, diræ obſcœnæque volucres,
Horrifico ſubitæ lapſu de montibus adſunt,
Diripiuntque dapes, laniant & cuncta rapaces.
165 Ex illo fluere, & retro ſublapſa referri
Omnia : nunc iterum mœrentia limina ſervant,
Infandum ! maleſuada Fames, & turpis Egeſtas.
   T U N C animum ſubiît legatum mittere certum
Tecta Jovis Patris, ſuperûm qui regnat in aulâ,
170 Aulicolaſque ſuos qui adeat, noſtroſque labores
Infandos memoret : ſic ſtat ſententia ; miſſus
Qui mandata ferat, ſupplex & voce precetur.
   " Summe Pater nobis miſeris ſuccurre, tuoque
   " Parce pio generi, & propiùs res aſpice noſtras
175 " Submerſas, fer opem præſens, opibuſque juvato :
   " Omnibus exhauſtas nos cladibus, omnium egenas,
   " Reſpicias ; neu priſca ſinas neglecta jacere
   " Atria ſacra tibi, nec paupertate Camœnas
   " Squalere infames. *Harpyias* pelle rapaces.
180   N E C mora, corripuit greſſus, mandata peregit
Legatus, votis noctuque diuque fatigat

                        " Auli-

Aulicolas cunctosque, Jovemque & plurimus ipsum.
Vota nec ingratâ aversus Pater optimus aure
Respuit ; ast statim jussit mandata referri
185 Auri ad custodes Quæstores : instat & urget
Legatus fidus, votis precibusque fatigat.
Verùm vota cadunt, heu! multa & inania nobis
Quæstores mandant tandem ædes inspiciendas,
Quo constet ratio sumptusque ac instaurandi :
190 At nihil ulterius ; speramus sed fore posthac.
Non vacat exiguis superis, heu! rebus adesse ;
Ingentes undæ rerum quæ mole laborant,
Extrudunt nostras : Musas nec respicit ullus.

    HINC quoque ad *Æthiopum* rapidus secesserat oras
195 Jupiter, extremos ultra Garamantas & Indos,
Non qui festa agitet lætus convivia, ut olim ;
Sed qui commotos possit componere fluctus
Oceani Australis, tempestatesque sonoras
Imperio premat ac vinclis & carcere frænet,
200 Disjectam & præsens toto levet æquore classem,
Quæ jam mole suâ ac immenso pondere mersa
Auri, ah! it pessum subito, ditatque profundum.
Forsan & hinc rediens, qui jam *Oxonam*que *Camum*que
Visit, nos viset languentis & ostia *Donæ.*
205   SPEMQUE metumque inter dubiæ transegimus annos
Hinc aliquot ; tandem nobis spes omnis adempta :
Aversos superos non nos curare putamus.
Suppliciter tristes, & tunsæ pectora palmis,
Multa diu nostro volventes pectore sæva,
210 Ibamus tacitæ pulcherrimæ ad ostia *Donæ,*
Et tandem dictis nostra ora resolvimus hisce.
   " RESPICE nos miseras, rapidis nos, *Dona,* fluentis
  " Obrue, & avectas *Nerei* sub cærula verras :
  " Seu tu, *Phœbe* Pater, qui conspicis omnia, & olim
215 " Huc tecum advectas subduxti, defer in altum,

" Nos-

" Nofque vehas iterum Permeffi ad flumina facri,
" Et juga Parnaffi, ne nos hîc turpis egeftas
" Oppimat, aut fubitò tollat nos fæva ruina,
" Dum collapfa ruunt fubductis tecta columnis.
220 " Præfentem nobis intentant omnia mortem.
" Nemo *Elphinftonii*, *Dunbari*, nemo *Stuarti*
" Exfurgit fimilis, nullus *Forbefius*, eheu!
" Scis hæc, *Phœbe* Pater; jam nos hinc defer in altum.
PROTINUS horrifico tonitru cælum omne remugit:
225 Ac veluti tripode ex facro vox fertur ad aures
Phœbi : nos placidâ folatus voce profatur.
" NON me prætereunt cafus veftrique labores,
" *Donaides* caræ : veftro quàm fæpe dolore
" Condolui? revocate animos mœftumque timorem
230 " Mittite, forfan & hæc olim meminiffe juvabit :
" O paffæ graviora, Deus dabit his quoque finem,
" Durate & vofmet rebus fervate fecundis.
" Huc ego vos duxi mecum, Jovis ipfa fecutus
" Juffa Patris fummi : fedem vos linquere nolim
235 " Antiquam & propriam, quam fpondent fata perennem.
" Refpiciet tandem (ni fallor) Jupiter æquus,
" Auxiliumque feret vobis, opibufque juvabit ;
" Efficietque, ut dira Fames & turpis Egeftas
" Exulet, & fugiant Harpyiæ trifte rapaces.
240 " Interea vobis (augur ni vanus Apollo)
" Eximius furget fautor qui veftra novabit
" Mœnia, quique finu tenero vos molle fovebit.
Annuit & *Phœbo* jam leni murmure *Dona*.
HIS animum arrectæ dictis, à flumine in ædes
245 Corripimus greffus : en nuncia litera nobis
Prævertens, multa ac ingentia dona ferebat,
FRASERII fignata manu, quæ furgere juffit
Muros, & cellas Pario de marmore Mufis.
Nec femel hoc factum eft ; en altera & altera venit
250 Litera, plura ferens ingentia munera nobis.

EIA

EIA alacres hilaresque Virum cantemus, & ampla
Dona, quibus nos accumulans onerârit amicus
FRASERIUS.   Triftes hâc tempeftate Camœnas
Solus refpexit, cum defertis *Aganippes*
255 Vallibus efuriens migraret in atria *Clio*,
Mufarum & nati nec fœdum aut turpe putarent
Præcones fieri, aut atros conducere furnos.
Cumque *Jovi* exiguis noftris, heu! rebus adeffe.
Non vacet; heu! Mufis *Mæcenas* nullus & adfit,
260 *Almam* nec *Matrem* refpectet filius ullus,
FRASERIUS folus refpexit lumine læto.
Atria Mufarum collapfa, jacentia tecta
Erigit, & fulcit fublimibus alta columnis
Arte laboratis mirâ: fplendefcere cuncta
265 Marmore nunc puro, vitreifque nitefcere quadris
Juffit, & innumeros *Mufæo* dona libellos
Intulit; hic donat, donavit, & ufque daturus.
Hinc *Elphinftonia*, aut hinc jam *Dunbaria* tecta
Fraferiana fonent: incifum marmora fervent
270 Nomen & arma viri: hunc & pictum monftret *Apelles*.
FRASERIUS mediis ftatuatur in ædibus ipfis,
Atque aliis monftrans non quæ jam erexerit ipfe,
Sed quæ nunc jaceant, aliisque ftruenda relinquat.
ECCE! ferunt Nymphæ calathis tibi lilia plenis
275 Cana, rofas violis miftas & fuave rubentes,
Carpunt & myrtos, ederas, laurofque comantes;
Hinc variis foliis intexunt ferta, caputque
Præcingunt duplici vittis auroque coronâ.
O bone FRASERI, Mufarum maxima cura,
280 Non opis eft noftræ grates perfolvere dignas:
Præmia digna ferant meritis tibi numina magnis,
Neftoreos annos, felicia fauftaque cuncta.
Nuda tibi virtus, mens & fibi confcia recti
Grata placet; nudam virtutem amplecteris ipfam;
285 Præmia non curas.   Quæ te tam læta tulerunt

Sæcula

Sæcula? qui tanti talem genuere parentes?
In freta dum fluvii current, dum montibus umbræ
Lustrabunt convexa, polus dum sidera pascet;
Semper honos, nomenque tuum laudesque manebunt.
290   E i a alacres hilaresque Virum tollamus in astra,
Cui Deus incoctum generoso pectus honesto
Indidit, & quem ardens evexit ad æthera virtus.
O bone F R A S E R I, pietate insignis ~~avità,~~
Di tibi divitias tribuerunt, Di tibi mentem
295 Munificam, proprios sapiens qui didis in usus.
A te divitiis uti jam discat avarus,
Qui loculis inhiat, congesto gaudet & auro.
Optime F R A S E R I, generose ac inclyte factis,
Quique modum rebus, certos & ponere fines,
300 Congruus ac almæ Naturæ vivere nosti,
Vive, vale felix, cuncta & tibi prospera vertant.

Scribebam ad ostia Donæ in viciniâ
Coll. Regii Aberdonen. A. D. 1725.
Mart. 25.   *I. K.*

F I N I S.

N O T.

NOTÆ
IN
DONAIDES.

Not. 1. *Verſ.* 3. *Atria Muſarum, &c.*] Ædes Collegii Regii A-
berdonenſis, de nomine JACOBI IV. *Scotorum* Regis ita
dicti, per complures annos exornatæ ſtabant benè ſartæ
tectæ.

2. v. 5.   *Elphinſtonius, &c.*] Florebant artium liberalium ſtudia in
Civitate veteri *Aberdonenſi,* intra pomoeria Canoniæ Eccle-
ſiæ Cathedralis, per ſæcula quædam ante erectam Univerſitatem. Hîc enim, ex quo *Murthlaco* ad *Donam* tranſlata fuit
Epiſcopalis ſedes à DAVIDE I. *Scotorum* Rege, circiter An.
1125, Canonici non ſolùm Theologiam, Jus cum Canonicum
tum Civile, ſed Grammaticam & Philoſophiam profitebantur
& docebant. Anno autem 1494, ſereniſſimus & auguſtiſſi-
mus JACOBUS IV. *Scotorum* Rex, exorato ALEXANDRO VI.
Romano Pontifice, Univerſitatem *Aberdonenſem* in inclytâ Civitate veteris *Aberdoniæ* (ſic ſe habent ipſa verba Diplomatis,
dati *Romæ,* 4 *Id. Feb.* 1494) fundandam & erigendam curavit, adminiſtrante clariſſimo *Gulielmo Elphinſtonio,* Epiſcopo *Aberdonenſi,* priùs ſummo Regni *Scotiæ* Cancellario, tunc
à ſecretiori Sigillo. Univerſitatem ab *Elphinſtonio* inſtitu-
tam, nec non Regiâ & Pontificiâ auctoritate ornatam omnibus artium liberalium profeſſionibus, omnibuſque poteſtatibus,
immunitatibus & privilegiis, quæ Univerſitati *Pariſienſi, Bo-
nonienſi, Aurelianenſi,* aut quibuſvis aliis ullibi conceſſa ſunt;
Rex JACOBUS, multis & variis terris, prædiis & reditibus
donavit, iis ſciz. univerſis & ſingulis quos olim tenebat Hoſ-
pitale Sancti *Germani* in *Laudonia* apud *Tranent,* Eccleſiâ de
Slaines, &c. ut liquet ex Regiâ ipſius Chartâ datâ *Sterlini* 19
Auguſti 1498, Chartiſque aliis. Egregiis quoque muneribus
illam affecit *Elphinſtonius* ipſe. Verùm permulta & præclara
Regis & *Elphinſtonii* merita, eaque omnia quæ ſpectant ad
primævam & optimam Univerſitatis inſtitutionem *Elphinſto-
nianam,*

nianam, bre itatis ergô hîc omittimus. Si quis fortè hæc aut id genus alia fo re cupiat, fufè enarrata cernet, fi in lucem unquam prodea t *Athenæ noftræ Aberdonenfes, & Archæologia noftra Aberdo enfis.*

3. *v.* 7.   *Regis de nomine dictam*] V. *Not.* 1 & 2. item, *Hect. Boet. Vit. Ep. Aberdonen.* Fol. 37. *Collegio, quod felicis memoriæ* Wilhelmus *tuus anteceffor R E G A L E voluit apellari.*

4. *v.* 31.   *Hector adeft*] *Hectorem Boetium* & *Gulielmum Haium, Taodunanos, Parifiis,* ubi Philofophiam profitebantur, *Aberdoniam* arceffivit Cl. *Elphinftonius,* ad jacienda Academiæ *Aberdonenfis* fundamenta in artibus liberalibus. V. *Hect. Boet. Vit. Ep. Aberd.* Fol. 27. *Hector* primus Collegii Regii creatus Principalis; *Haiufque* primus Subprincipalis. *Hector* fcripfit infignem rerum *Scoticarum* Hiftoriam; *Haius* verò Prælectiones Theologicas: quas MStâs carie fituque obductas, inter fcruta Bibliothecæ latitantes, nos nuper de novo compactas Almæ Matri poftliminio reddidimus. Verum de *Hectoris* & *Haii* fcriptis & factis, fufè nos *Athen. Aberdon.*

5. *v.* 33.   *Nomina docta*] Viri literis infignes, qui communi *Boetii* & *Haii* operâ inftituti, è Collegio Regio *Aberdonenfi* prodiêrunt ante An. 1521: *Alexander Haius,* Rector Univerfitatis; *Jacobus Ogilvæus,* J. Civ. P. *Arthurus Boethius,* J. Can. D. *Jo. Adamus,* S. Th. D. *&c.* Hos recenfet ipfe *Hector,* Vit. Ep. *Ab.* Fol. 28. His adjecimus nos duos eximios viros ab *Hectore* omiffos, *Joan. Vaufium* & *Rob. Graium;* hunc Medicum, illum rei Grammaticæ peritiffimum. *Ath. Aberd.*

6. *v.* 35.   *Carolus & Magnus*] Univerfitatem *Parifienfem* fub *Carolo* Magno condidere *Scoti,* ab *Achaio* Rege miffi, *Joannes Scotus, Claudius Clemens, Rabanus Maurus* & *Flaccus Albinus,* V. *Spotfwod. Hift.* p. 22. *Hect. Boet. Hift.* Fol. 195. *Joan. Leflæi Hift.* Lib. 5, p. 167. P. *Abercromb. Mart. Fact. Scot.* Vol. 1. p. 118. *Geo. Mackenz. Vit.* Vol I. Univerfitatem *Aberdonenfem* condidere *Scoti* quidem; aft Almæ Matris *Parifienfis* Alumni. *Jod. Bad.* in Ep. Nuncupatoriâ de Grammaticâ *Joan. Vauf.* An. 1522. Vide quoque *Not.* 4. Atque ita *Scotiæ* quam acceptam referebat gratiam *Gallia* rependit.

7 *v.* 36.   *Poft Elphinftonium Dunbari*] Extincto Cl. *Elphinftonio,* An. 1514, omnibus probis multùm defiderato, Antiftes *Aberdonenfis* creatus eft *Alexander Gordonius,* quem ex antiqua *Gordoniorum* de H A D D O gente oriundum, virumque pium accepimus.

cepimus. Cùm autem is adversâ valetudine uteretur per annum unum & alterum, & tandem fato functus esset, suffectus est Cl. *Gavinus Dunbarus,* Anno 1518. Is amplissimo usus patrimonio, (quippe qui haberet patrem *Alexandrum,* cui primò data fuit à Rege hæreditaria provinciæ Moraviensis Præfectura juridica, seu Vicecomitatus, ut vulgò loquuntur, aliique honores, cum variis prædiis & reditibus, cuique jure hæreditario cùm insignia tum bona ipsius Comitatùs Moraviensis cedere oportebat) ne teruncium quidem ex universo censu Episcopatûs *Aberdonen.* quem per tredecim annos gessit, in privatum sui suorumque commodum contulit, sed totum & integrum in pios usus erogavit; quæ in Collegio nondum ad finem ducta essent, perfecit. Augustiora quidem Collegii opera molienda curaverat *Elphinstonius;* templum in primis construxit, egregiè ornatum, multáque pretiosâ supellectili instructam; Campanile sublime & excelsum coronario ornavit opere maxime insigni; unde Imperiale Diadema, lapideis arcubus suffultum, supra plumbeam tecturam, latè conspicuum fulget: Aulas quoque duas, alteram inferiorem, alteram superiorem, magnificam sane, reliquasq; omnes Collegii ædes, præter eas quæ sunt ad areæ latus australe, exstruendas curavit. Juris Canonici quoque, Juris Civilis, Medicinæ & Grammatices Professoribus singulis singulas ædes, (*Mansiones* vulgò vocant) cùm hortis, terris, glebis, aliisque pertinentibus, habitandi simul docendi causâ, à Collegio secretas designavit, & designatas exstruebat: verùm has non absolvit, morte correptus intempestivâ. Eas Mansiones, ut & Collegii latus australe, consummavit *Dunbarus. Dunbaria* hæc tecta renovari cœperunt An. 1707, columnarum ordine decorata pulchro; sed deficiente pecuniâ huc usque neglecta jacent. Verùm nunc columnas erigi, & tecta supernè partim provehi jubet munificentissimus noster JACOBUS FRASERIUS. *Gavinus* quoque primævam Universitatis institutionem *Elphinstonianam* summo cum labore edendam curavit. Obiit 6 *Id.* *Martii,* 1531, *Andreapoli.*

&. v. *ib.*   *Sacra Stuarti insula*] An. 1532, *Gulielmus Stuartus* ad Episcopatum *Aberdon.* & proinde Universitatis Cancellariatum evectus est. Hic Antistes præclarus, *Elphinstonio & Dunbari* haud dissimilis, neque prius neque antiquius quicquam habuit, quàm ut Academiam augeret & ornaret; pomœria Collegii

legii, & ab Orientali parte & à Boreali, ampliora fecit. Hîc
ædes quafdam prope templum Collegii Regii Capellanis Cho-
ri exftrui juffit;' Bibliothecam, · Veftiario Templi fuperftru-
ctam, lapide polito & plumbeo tecto ornandam curavit ; ut
& eodem modo fupernè ornavit & texit Gazophylacium, feu
Cimeliarchium (Jocalium, aut Chartarum domus, vel The-
fauraria vulgò dicitur) & Capitulum, feu domum Capitula-
rem, ubi publica Collegii Comitia haberi folebant. Bibliothecam longitudine duplò fere auctam, hafque tres ædes modò
dictas, Bibliothecæ fubjectas, nunc in quatuor Scholas divifas,
quæ Templo contiguæ, Collegii Regii aream ad Aquilo-
nem claudunt, ab imis fundamentis polito lapide pulcherrimum in modum exftruendas curavit generofus Mufarum cultor & fautor nofter JACOBUS FRASERIUS, An. 1724. Verùm de præclaris aliis *Dunbari* & *Stuarti* factis, nos affatim,
Ath. Aberd.

9. v. 46. *Orta eft, Gordonio*] An. 1546, Præful *Aberdonenfis* renun-
ciatus eft *Gulielmus Gordonius*, è nobiliffima *Gordoniorum* de
HUNTLEY familia natus, at moribus ab illo *Gordonio* priùs
memorato longè diverfus. Is initio Pontificatûs fui bonum
Antiftitem præ fe ferebat, & ob literas bene audiebat : verum
brevi, feu fœdâ libidinum proluvie immerfus, uti vulgò fertur,
feu odio inftauratæ Religionis ductus, ampliffimos Ecclefiæ *A-
berdonen.* cenfus ad vilem ferè affem redegiffe dicitur ; re verâ
comprobans quod in ore habuiffe fertur, *Se ex his reditibus facris, quod vix Presbytero Genevenfi fufficeret, relicturum.* Quædam etiam prædia ab *Elphinftonio* Almæ Matri facrata ab-
alienavit. Mortuus eft An. 1577.

10. v. 54. *Honos, Leflæ, manebit*] Hic eft ille *Joannes Leflæus*, fa-
cundus rerum *Scoticarum* fcriptor, fide fuâ in MARIAM Re-
ginam nobilis. Sub *Gordonio* florebat, J. Can. P. in Collegio
Regio, deinde Epifcopus *Roffenfis* creatus. Obiit *Bruxellis*,
An. 1596. *Leflæo* etiam æquales floruerunt in Collegio Regio viri literis infignes, *Joannes Biffat, Alexander Anderfonus*, uterque S. Th. P. & Collegii Principalis ; *Nicolaus Haius*,
J. Civ. P. *Theoph. Stuartus*, Grammaticus ; *Joan. Henderfonus,
Rob. Metellanus*, aliique Regentes. Inter alumnos Collegii
Regii tunc temporis maximè infignes fuerant, *Jac. Chynæus*
de *Arnage*, Mathefeos Profeffor apud *Duacenos*, & *Gulielmus
Barclaius* celeberrimus Jurifconfultus, clariffimi *Joannis Bar-
claii*

claii Pater. Hîc autem *Alexandrum Gallovidianum*, Canonicum *Aberdonensem*, & Ecclesiæ *Kinkeldensis* Rectorem, silentio præterire piaculum duco. Eximio huic viro, doctrinâ claro, probitate & fide spectatissimo, quicquid hodie novimus de antiquâ re Ecclesiasticâ *Aberdonensi*, totum fere acceptum referendum est. Hujus labore improbo & impensis, Chartularia quæ in Collegio Regio exstant, ex antiquioribus Regiftris confecta funt : In monumentis quoque Collegii clariffimus. Floruit fub quatuor Epifcopis *Aberdonenfbus*, *Elphinftonio*, *Dunbaro*, *Stuarto* & *Gordonio*. Sub exeuntem *Elphinftonii* Pontificatum, omnia Pontificis negotia ipfius ductu adminiftrata, ut & per totum *Dunbari* Epifcopatum. In exftruendis Collegii ædibus, aliifque facris, & in ponte *Deenfi* condendo, magnam impendit operam. *H. Boet.* Vit. Ep. *b.* Fol. 27 & 38. Florente *Stuarto*, affeffor fuit in vifitatio ne Univerfitatis habita An. 1542. Sub *Gordonio* ipfe Rector fuit Univerfitatis, An. 1549. De viro autem hoc egregio, aliifque viris hîc nominatis, fufiùs diximus *Ath. Aberd.*

11. *v.* 56.   *Heu ! pia gens nimium*] Purioris religionis vindices, eamque inftaurandi ftudium maximopere laudamus ; ardorem autem, ædes SUMMO NUMINI aut Mufis facratas diripiendi & demoliendi, vix laudandum cenfemus.

12. *v.* 58.   *Sacrato Templo*] Templo Collegii Regii *Aberdonen.*

13. *v.* 62.   *Andreades*] *Alexander Anderfonus*, ultimus Collegii Regii Principalis ante inftauratam religionem, qui cum plebs *Merniensis* Ecclefiam Cathedralem *Aberdonenfem* tecto plumbeo fpoliatam diripuiffet, & continuò ad templum Collegii Regii, reliquafque ædes Mufis facratas diripiendas devolaret, forti manu vim vi repellere nititur ; audacem fortunâ juvante, integra & intacta huc ufque manent augufta Mufarum tecta. *Anderfonus* hic, unâ cum Subprincipali & Regentibus, quòd Papanis ritibus mordicus hærentes, Confeffionem Fidei & doctrinæ purioris, Comitiorum regni legibus fancitam amplecti recufarent, officiis fuis privati funt An. 1569. V. *Petr. Hift. Eccl.* Cent. 16, p. 362. & *Jo. Lefl.* Lib. 10. p. 530.

14. *v.* 63.   *Noftra quoque Archiva fervata*] Ex his Archivis *Aberdon.* quæ huc ufque exftant, & ex primæva Univerfitatis *Aberd.* inftitutione *Elphinftoniana* (quæ optima habetur, & rei antiquæ apud S C O R O S ftudiofis magni ducitur) certiffima fere nunc hauriri poteft notitia antiqui Academiarum *Scoticarum*

fta-

status ante instauratam religionem; cum sub id tempus, U-
niversitas *Andreana* & *Glascuana* magnam Diplomatum &
Chartarum fecerint jacturam. Hinc ortum ceperunt *Athenæ*
nostræ *Aberd.*

15. *v.* 64. *Regales Chartas, multa & Diplomata*] Quæ exstant in
Chartophylacio Coll. Regii.

16. *v.* 65. *Nec tamen—finis fuit ille malorum*] Quanquam Almæ Matri ædes suæ intactæ, & Archiva quoque integra manserint,
haud leve damnum passa est sub instauratæ religionis tempus;
abrogatâ optimâ celeberrimi *Elphinstonii* Institutione Universitatis primævâ, & substitutâ Institutione novâ, (*Fundatio-
nem novam* vulgò vocant) quæ prodiit An. 1592, sub hoc
titulo, *COLLEGIUM REGALE ABERDONENSE*,
institutum, reformatum & restitutum, in modum Erectionis
novæ paulò ante præscriptæ Academiis *Andreanæ* & *Glascu-
anæ*, & unde maximam partem exscripta videtur Erectio
Collegii *Mareschallani* anno sequenti 1593. Institutio hæc
nova, (cujus Auctor fuit *David Rhætus*, Coll. Regii Principalis) eò sane multo melior quòd Papanos tollat ritus: in
aliis autem plerisque omnibus, veterem *Elphinstonianam* præ-
ferendam censemus. Utramque fusiùs collatam dedimus, *Ath.
Aberd.*

17. *v.* 67. *Exiliumque Themis patitur*] Ex Institutione hâc novâ,
rejectæ sunt, ut parum utiles, professiones Juris Canonici,
Juris Civilis, Medicinæ & Musices, olim ab *Elphinstonio* in-
stitutæ.

18. *v.* 79. *Jacobus Sextus*] Summus ille Musarum cultor & fautor
Regius, perpendens antiquos census & reditus, qui olim quidem, pro temporis ratione, alendis Collegii membris satis e-
rant; tunc autem, crescente indies rerum venalium pretio,
iisdem sustentandis nullo pacto sufficere; Academiam Regiam summis auxit muneribus. Huic concessit & donavit, An.
1574, omnes decimas, feuda, proventusque Ecclesiæ *Turvi-
ensis*, *Carmelitanorum* Fratrum de *Bamff*, Ecclesiæ Divi *Pe-
tri* de *Spittal* (h. e. contractè pro *Hospital*) seu Subcanto-
riæ *Aberdonen.* & Capellaniarum *Westhallensis* & *Folarulen-
sis*. Anno autem 1579, Decanatum Ecclesiæ Cathedralis *A-
berdonen.* h. e. integros reditus Ecclesiæ Parochialis S. *Macarii*, quæ jam tripartita est in has Ecclesias, Veterem *Macarii*,

No-

Novam *Macarii*, & illam de *Newhills*: Anno vero 1586, omnes decimas reditusque Ecclesiæ *Methlicensis.*

19 *v.*82. *Hîc Metelane— Arbuthnote— Stuarte*] Secundùm Regem J a c o b u m, omni amore profequendi funt tres egregii viri, quibus regias donationes modò memoratas acceptas refert Alma Mater: *Robertus Metellanus,* Decanus *Aberdon.* poftea in fupremâ Curiâ apud *Scotos* Senator; *Alexander Arbuthnotus & Walterus Stuartus,* optimi Coll. Regii Principales. De eximiis his viris egimus, *Athen. Aberd.*

20. *v.*85. *Harpyias avidas*] Regiis J a c o b i donationibus, per annos complures frui non licuit per *Harpyias avidas,* tunc omnia bona Collegii Regii diripientes, aut turpiter fœdantes. Per *Harpyias* hîc intelligendi funt illi, quibus Manfiones Profefforum Juris Canonici, Juris Civilis, Medicinæ & Grammatices, cum hortis & prædiis tunc temporis in feudum dimiffæ funt, & quibus damnofæ multarum terrarum aliarum, Coll. Regio facrarum, locationes faftæ funt per *Davidem Rhætum* aliofque. *Rhætus* hic, literarum quidem ftudiis haud fpernendus; aliàs autem non adeò bene audit. Hîc ad rem fuam nimis attentus, in re communi Coll. Regii procurandâ parum fidus perhibetur. Ipfe ab Anno 1592, ad Annum 1619, & Principalis & communis Procurator, omnia arbitrio fuo adminiftrabat folus ferè, abfque confilio reliquorum Moderatorum Academiæ, queis jure debetur communis adminiftrandi provincia. Omnia tunc peffum ibant; languebant miferum in modum Mufæ; tefta *Athenæi* fœdè neglefta jacebant; Profeffores artium & V. D. Præcones, ftipendia non perfoluta querebantur: Cum Mufis, virtus & religio ipfa exulabat; ad ipfas portas Ecclefiæ Cathedralis invalefcebant Pagani ritus. Hæc difertim teftantur afta Vifitationis Regiæ, habitæ An. 1619 à clariffimo *Patricio Forbefio,* Epifcopo *Aberdon.*

21. *v.*87. *Donec Patricius, &c.*] An. 1618, exortum eft fulgentiffimum illud fidus, Academiæ Regiæ ufque præfens & propitium, celeberrimus *Pat. Forbefius à Corfe.* Is, pofthabitâ Fundatione novâ, primævam Univerfitatis Inftitutionem *Elphinftonianam* poftliminio reftituendam curavit per Delegatos ab J a c o b o VI. An. 1619, & tandem fupremis Regni Comitiis fanciendam, An. 1633, quæ huc ufque apud nos viguit, vigetque. Hinc rediêrunt Profeffiones Juris Canonici, Juris

Ci-

Civilis, Medicinæ & Mufices. Novam etiam S. Th. Profeffio-
nem inftituit.   Quantum autem Ecclefiam *Aberdon.* Epifcopus hic, quantum Univerfitatem *Aberdon.* Cancellarius hic
auxerit & ornârit, dicere in proclivi non eft : Almam Matrem jacentem attollens, ulnifque amplexus benignus fovit ;
artus collapfos & amputata Membra mirâ dexteritate unit,
medicâque manu fanos & integros reftituit.   Illi ædes quas
incoleret inftaurandas, cenfum & annuos reditus quibus ale-
retur, partim redimendos, partim confirmandos, fummo cum
labore curat.   Cuncta quæ nuper tenebris, fitu & torpore
fqualebant, erexit & correxit, luce & calore fuo vitali corufca
& vegeta effecit.   Exinde effœta Mater juvenefcere, fœcunda
natorum progenies fobolefcere, languentes Mufæ revivifcere,
& torpentia liberalium artium ftudia hîc iterum revirefcere
cœperunt.   Ita hujus aufpiciis nata eft aurea illa ætas literarum *Aberdon.* in quâ floruerunt viri egregiè docti & pii, præ-
fulgidæ ftellæ ex aureo hoc fidere ortæ.   De his V. *Not.* 24.

22 v. 103 *Patricio exftincto*] Obîit An. 1635. Quàm defideratiffimus
autem obîerit, indicio funt Orationes, Conciones, Elogia, E-
piftolæ, Poemata in primis elegantiffima Latina & Vernacula, collecta in Volumen unum in *Quarto,* & typis mandata
ab *Edwardo Rabano, Abredeæ,* 1635.   Num tale exftet mo-
nimentum literarium de obitu alicujus unius viri, Principis,
aut privati, nos latet.

23 v. 117 *Huic facimus tumulum*] Volumen hoc collectitium, quod
infcribitur, *Tumulus Reverendiffimi Patris PAT. FORBE-
SII à Corfe, Epifcopi Aberdon.* fummâ curâ digeftum, mo-
nimentum marmore & ære perennius, edendum curavit Cl.
Jo. Forbefius filius; quod locum dedit huic elegantiffimo *Artb.
Johnftoni* Epigrammati.

> *FORBESIOS bîc cerne duos, fine compare Patrem*
> *Et Natum, fecli fidus utrumque fui.*
> *Ante dedit vitam Nato Pater, omine læto,*
> *Nunc Patrem Nati vivere cernis ope.*
> *Plus meruit Natus; quam cepit clauditur ævo,*
> *Quam dedit annorum limite vita caret.*

24 v. 119 *Verùm orta ex aureo— lumina fidere clara*] Viri literis &
virtute infignes; in his Coryphæi, *Jo. Forbefius* à *Corfe, Rob.
Baronius, Alex. Scrogæus, Gul. Leflæus, Jac. Sibbaldus, A-
lex. Roffius,* S. Th. Doctores; domi forifque celeberrimi,
An.

An. 1638, aliique complures per totam Diœcesin *Aberdonen.* rerum sacrarum Mystæ doctissimi. Præter Theologos, florebant hi JCti, *Tho. Nicolsonus, Rogerus Mowætus, Jac. Sandilandius* senior, *Jac. Sandilandius* junior: Hi Medici; *Arthurus Johnstonus,* Medicus Regius, Poeta quoque elegantissimus; *Gulielmus Johnstonus, Pat. Dunæus, Gul. Gordonius.:* Hi Regentes, præter alios, eruditissimi, *And. Strachanus,* Philosophiæ Pr. *David Leochæus,* Græcarum Literarum Pr. Hi rei Grammaticæ, & Human. L. Pr. peritissimi; *David Wedderburnus* & *Joan. Lundæus.* Florebant & tunc temporis duo fratres, Coll. Regii alumni, *Tho. Rhædus,* Jacobo VI. à secretis in linguâ Latinâ, & *Alex. Rhædus,* Regius Caroli I. Medicus; & inter primos memorandi, *Gul. Forbesius,* S. Th. D. primus apud *Edinenses Episcopus;* & clarissimus *Robertus Gordonius à Straloch.* De universis & singulis dictum, *Athen. Aberd.*

25 v.121   *Linquis, Pater optime, natum*] Is est modò dictus celeberrimus *Jo. Forbesius à Corse,* auctor *Instructionum Historico-Theologicarum,* quem Pater *Patricius* primum in Coll. Regio S. Th. Professorem instituit.

26 v.124   Carolus *hinc primus*] Abrogato Episcoporum ordine apud *Scotos,* An. 1641, Carolus I. integros Ecclesiæ Episcopalis *Aberdon.* reditus Universitati *Aberdon.* sacravit: hinc duas partes sortitum est Coll. Regium, tertiam verò Coll. *Marischallanum.*

27 v.129   *Unde novas-- arces*] An. 1658, ex reditibus his sacris, summo studio erigendas curârunt Academiæ Moderatores ædes illas præaltas & insignes, quæ quadrangulari formâ ad Orientem æstivum, Templo & Aulæ communi contiguæ eminent, sex tabulatis altæ, viginti quatuor cubiculis instructæ, & turri sublimi, plumbarii operis, de tecturâ planâ plumbeâ surgente ornatæ. Ad ædes has exstruendas pecuniam quoq; contulerunt plurimi generosi & munificentissimi viri, ipsi etiam Academiæ Moderatores. De his nos diximus, *Ath. Aberd.*

Florebant tunc temporis in Coll. Regio viri literis insignes, *Joan. Rowæus,* Principalis, linguarum Latinæ in primis, & Hebraicæ doctus; *Gul. Duglassius,* S. T. P. *Jac. Sandilandius,* J. Civ. P. *Andræas Muir,* M. D. & P. *Pat. Sandilandius,* Subprincipalis; *Joan. Brodie,* H. L. P. quem excepit *Joan. Forbesius,* Elegantiæ Pr. eruditus; *Joan. Strachanus,*

D   *And.*

And. Maſſy & *Gul. Jobnſtonus,* Regentes Philoſ. Profeſſores.
Stracbano huic ingenii acutiſſimo, ſuffectus eſt *Geo. Gordonius,* perantiquâ *Gordoniorum* de HADDO gente oriundus, qui
poſtea Comes de ABERDEEN creatus eſt, & ſummus *Scotiæ*
Cancellarius. Sub idem tempus, aut non multò ante, pro-
dîit è Coll. Regio alumnus inſignis, JCtus celeberrimus D.
Geo. Mackenzæus, Advocatus Regius. *Andreæ Muir* Me-
dico ſuffectus eſt gener ſuus *Pat. Urquhartus,* M: D. & P.
qui per 53 annos officio ſummâ cum laude functus, etiamnum
vivit valetque 83 agens annum. Hoc florente, plurimi inſi-
gni Doctoris gradu in Medicinâ ornati, præter exteros & *An-
glos,* in queis Cl. *Seidenbammi* filius, & complures ex Socie-
tate Regiâ *Londinenſi;* apud *Scotos,* celeberrimus *Arch. Pit-
carnius, Joan. Drummondus, Geo. Chynæus, Tho. Boërus, Ja.
Keilus, Geo. Mackenzæus, Pat. Abercrombius,* nobiliſſimus
& doctiſſimus *Arch. Campbellus,* Comes de *Ilay, &c.*

28 *v.* 131   *Quos & reddidimus*] An. 1661, reſtituto CAROLO II. re-
ſtituti ſunt Epiſcopo *Aberdon.* ſui reditus, & Coll. Regio do-
natio facta eſt redituum ex Eccleſiis, ſi quæ fortè intra ſe-
ptennium vacarent in Diœceſi *Aberdon. Moravien. &c.* Verùm inde haud multum emolumenti provenit.

29 *v.* 134   *Aurantius beros*] An. 1695, Illuſtriſſimus GULIELMUS *Bri-
tanniæ* Rex, Palladis cùm ſagatæ tum togatæ cultor & fautor,
conceſſit trecentas libras Sterlinenſes Univerſitati *Aberdonenſi,*
(ut & tantundem *Andreanæ, Glaſcuanæ* & *Edinenſi*) annuatim ſolvendas ex Epiſcopatuum *Scoticorum* reditibus, cum quo
debita diſſolverentur, &, ære alieno conflato liberaretur U-
niverſitas, tum quò S. Th. Profeſſori, & S. Th. ſtudioſis pro-
ſpectum foret. Hinc centum libras ſortitum eſt Coll. *Mariſ-
challanum,* unde aucta ſunt Profeſſorum ſtipendia; ducentas
Coll. Regium, unde hodie cadunt Ling. Orient. Profeſſori libræ 66, aſſes 2, den. 2. 8--12. S. Th. Profeſ. 33 libræ, 6 aſſes,
8 den. Principali, 20 libræ; reliquumque duobus S. Th. ſtu-
dentibus, & communi Academiæ commodo inſervit.

30 *v.* 136   *Anna pia*] An. 1712, Sereniſſima ANNA Regina, cum
priùs ad illam ſuprema & ultima Regni *Scotici* Comitia, habita An. 1706, tenues *Scoticarum* Academiarum reditus, &
in primis exigua Profeſſorum ſtipendia, tabellis ſupplicibus de-
tuliſſent, donavit Univerſitati *Aberdon.* ducentas & decem libras ex Ærario ſuo *Scotico* annuatim ſolvendas, ad augenda
Pro-

(23)

Professorum stipendia: dimidia pars Coll. *Marischallano* obtigit. Ex centum & quinque libris quæ Coll. Regio cadunt, Principalis 20 libras, S. Th. P. 12 accipit; reliquas 73 libras æquis portionibus sortiuntur quatuor Regentes, (tres *sciz.* Phil. Professores, & unus Græcarum literarum Pr.) atq; Medicinæ, Grammatices & Juris Civ. Professores.

31 *v.* 137 --- *renovavit* GEORGIUS] Donum ANNÆ renovatum, confirmavit Augustissimus & Potentissimus GEORGIUS REX, privato suo Sigillo, An. 1719.

32 *v.* 139 *Privati quidam-- afficiunt donis*] Ad instauranda *sciz. Dunbaria* tecta. Vide *Not.* 7, sub finem. In his princeps *Joan. Buchanus* Chiliarcha, prisca *Buchanorum* de *Auchmacoy* familia oriundus. Hujus & cohortis suæ Præfectorum auspiciis, jacta sunt fundamenta pulchri istius operis novi à parte Australi areæ Collegii nostri, An. 1707. Huic etiam & illis acceptum referendum est, quòd ingens Aula nostra camerata novis fenestris amplis, novoque pavimento renovata sit An. 1724.

33 *v.* 146 *Teque tuumque natum, Scugalle*] Inter hos qui Bibliothecam Coll. Regii libris ornârunt, facilè principes sunt venerandus Pater, *Pat. Scugallus*, Episcopus *Aberd.* & optimo patre filius dignissimus Mr. *Henricus Scugallus. Henricus* hic eruditissimus & pientissimus vir, florente juventâ abreptus, desideratissimus obiit An. 1678, ætatis suæ 28, cùm per quadriennium in Coll. Regio Philosophiam, totidemque annis ibidem SS Th. professus fuisset, unius anni interstitio quò Ecclesiæ *Auchterlessensis* Pastorem agebat. Tabulis supremis S. Th. Professori in Coll. Regio quinquies mille minas Scoticanas, & Bibliothecæ libros suos omnes sacravit: hos libros, pater filio superstes, bonâ fide tradidit unà cum suis An. 1682. Præter hos plurimi alii Bibliothecam libris donârunt; quos silentii sipario obvolvamus oportet; quorundam tamen insigniorum nomina notabo. Præter antiquos, Cl: *Elphinstonium, Gul. Stuartum, Hect. Boetium, Joan. Vausium, &c.* ab instauratâ religione, libros dònârunt hi sequentes: *Alex. Rhædus*, Medicus Regius, libros suos omnes medicos, duosq; Globos, An. 1631. *And. Strachanus*, S. Th. D. & P. suos cunctos legavit, An. 1634. Mr. *Gul. Rhætus*, An. 1635. Mr. *Th. Mercerus*, civis *Abredeensis*, An. 1635. *Jacobus* Vicecomes de *Frendraught*, Dominus *Crichton*, An. 1643. D. *Franciscus Gordonius*, An. 1643. *Alex. Hamilton*, An. 1648. *A-lex.*

lex. Blackhall, H. L. P. in *Southwark*, An. 1649 & 1658.
Mr. *Geo. Clark*, V. D. M. An. 1656. Mr. *Geo. Anderson*,
An. 1658. *Gul. Duglaſſius*, S. Th. P. An. 1665. Mr. *Tho.
Sandilandius* à *Crabſtone*, libros juridicos, An. 1678. *Matth.
Mackail*, M. D. An. 1696. *Joan. Gordon*, Paſtor *Banchori-
enſis*, An. 1702. Mr. *Tho. Garden*, V. D. M. An. 1720.
Jac. Burnetus, J. U. D. An. 1720 & 1723. *Jac. Fraſeri-
us*, J. U. D. An. 1723. Hi tres ultimi, *Fraſerius, Garde-
nius* & *Burnetus*, unà cum duobus primis, *Al. Rhædo* & *And.
Strachano*, maximâ ſecundum *Scugallos* Bibliothecam libro-
rum copiâ ornârunt.

34 *v.* 149   *Hîc quoque, qui Burſas donârunt*] Viri pio in Ecclefiam &
Rempub. ſtudio ducti, qui alendis artium liberalium ſtudiofis
bono ingenio præditis, inopiâ autem rei familiaris laboranti-
bus, terras aut pecuniam facrârunt : *Th. Burnetus* à *Leyes*, E-
ques Baron. alendis tribus ſtudiofis quædam prædia inter pomœria Civitatis *Abredeenſis* donavit, An. 1648. Mr. *Ja. Wattus*, V. D. M. in agro *Eboracenſi*, alendo uni, quædam præ-
diola in viciniâ Civitatis *Aberdonenſis* dedit, An. 1623. *Walt.
Ogilvæus* de *Redhyth*, integras fuas terras de *Redhyth*, ad a-
lendos 20 ſtudiofos, quorum 12 Grammaticæ in Scholâ *For-
dicianâ*, & 8 Philofophiæ in Coll. Regio operam navarent,
tabulis fuis legavit, An. 1678. Mr. *Geo. Melvillus*, V. D. M.
de *Alford*, alendis tribus legavit ter mille minas Scoticanas An.
1678. Mr. *Jac. Park*, V. D. M. de *Urquhart*, alendis duobus,
bis mille minas legavit, An. 1691. Eodem An. *Alex. Adamus*,
M. D. alendis tribus, terras quafdam fuburbanas, unà cum
domo & horto in urbe *Abredeenſi* conceſſit. Mr. *Jac. Fullar-
tonius, Halſtadæ* in *Angliâ* Ludimagiſter, alendis decem, fex-
centas fexaginta libras Anglicanas tabellis fuis legavit, An.
1692. Hinc comparati funt fundi in *Aberdoniæ* fuburbano.
Mr. *Gul. Watſon*, V. D. M. *Leſlæenſis*, alendis duobus legavit bis mille minas, An. 1699. *Margareta Gordonia*, è prifcâ
familiâ *Lefmorenſi* nata, conjux Comarchi de *Braco*, opulen-
tiſſimæ *Dufforum* gentis Principis, alendo uni donavit mille
libras Scoticanas, An. 1706. D. *Alex. Falconerus* de *Glen-
farquhar*, alendis quatuor, trecentas & viginti libras annuatim folvendas tabellis fuis legavit, An. 1716. Poſtremò, *Jo.
Greggus*, Mercator *Aberdon.* alendo uni mille libras fupremis tabellis deſtinavit, An. 1724. Præter hos, alii etiam a-
lia

lia in eundem finem deſtinârunt, *Alex. Rhædus*, M. D. An.
1636, *Joan. Lorimer*, An. 1673, Comarchus de *Udney*, &c.
Verùm inde modò nil emolumenti percipit Collegium.

35 *v.* 158   *Nec tamen interea res ſalva eſt noſtra*] Nec tamen muneribus G u l. Regis, A n n æ Reginæ, aut privatorum quorundam, res ſubmerſæ Collegii Regii peſſum euntes, emer-
gere valebant, has præſertim ob cauſas: Auguſta *Elphinſtonii* tecta, temporis edacis injuriâ, caſum triſteſque ruinas
minitabantur; Coronarium in primis illud opus inſigne & ex-
celſum, Campanili impoſitum, hiatus latè pandens, ſecum in
exitium tracturum Templum, Bibliothecam, Principalis ca-
meram. Jamque *Dunbaria* tecta, partim ſolo æquata, partim jamjam caſura nutabant. Jamque iterum Harpyiæ diræ
& rapaces adſunt, Muſis cibaria ſua abripientes: per *Harpyias*
hoc loco intellige hæreditarios prædiorum poſſeſſores, quibus, *Scotorum* legibus nuperis, decimas æſtimare licet, nec
non V. D. Præcones, queis ſtipendia augeri ex decimis qui-
buſcunque iiſdem legibus conceſſum eſt. Hinc nuper pluri-
mum imminuti ſunt Collegio regio reditus antiqui & priſci,
quos ab ipſis incunabulis Univerſitatis jure tenebat. Inde eſt
quòd Profeſſoribus ſtipendia ſint admodum exigua; nec longè abſit *maleſuada fames, & turpis egeſtas.* Hâc de cauſâ
Profeſſor Matheſeos, doctiſſimus *Tho. Boërus*, ante annos a-
liquot deſeruit Collegium. Hoc & alii meditantur, ſi qua
melior ſors obveniat.

36 *v.* 168   *Tunc animum ſubiit legatum, &c.*] An. 1718, miſſus eſt
Mr. *Geo. Chalmers* Principalis, ad Sereniſſimum G e o r g i u m
Regem, qui infandos Coll. Regii labores memoret, ſupplexq;
Athenæo Regio opes Regias oret. Quanquam per ingentes
undas rerum, immenſas præſertim *Oceani Auſtralis*, res mole ſuâ laborantes, huc uſque vota noſtra exaudita non ſint;
indies porro exauditum iri ſperamus.

37 *v.* 174   *Parce pio generi*] Profeſſoribus in Majeſtatem tuam Regiam piis & bene affectis.

38 *v.* 178   *Atria ſacra tibi*] Coll. Regium, quod J a c o b u m IV. &
ipſius Auguſtiſſimos Succeſſores Patronos ſibi vendicat.

39 *v.* 189   *Quo conſtet ratio ſumptuſque ac inſtaurandi*] Verſui huic
Spondaico & tardo, non ineptus videtur locus; *Voti non com-
pos, languet inops Muſa.*

40 v. 194   *Hinc quoque ad Æthiopum, &c.*] Alluditur ad *Hom. Iliad.*
1. *v.* 423.

Ζεὺς γὰρ ἐπ᾽ ὠκεανὸν μετ᾽ ἀμύμονας Ἀιθιοπῆας
Χθιζὸς ἔβη μετὰ δαῖτα.———

41 v. 203   *Forsan & hinc rediens*] Forsan Rex GEORGIUS, rediens
ab *Oceano Australi,* (h. e. compositis ingentibus undis rerum)
respiciet tandem languentes Musas *Aberdonenses;* sicuti re-
spexit *Oxonienses* & *Cantabrigienses,* qui has amplis donis
bonus & propitius jam cumulârit.

42 v. 210   *Ibamus tacitæ*] Alluditur ad *Hom l.* 1. *v.* 34.

Βῆ δ᾽ ἀκέων παρὰ θῖνα πολυφλοίσβοιο θαλάσσης.

43 v. 224   *Protinus horrifico tonitru*] Tonitrus & fulgur interdum fau-
sti ominis sunt, *Virg. Æn.* 2, 693, *Intonuit lævum. Hom. l.*
2, 353, Ἀστράπλων ἐπιδέξι, ἐναίσιμα σήμαλα φαίνων. Innui-
tur hîc Jovem probare dicta sequentia Phœbi, & rata fore
quæ *DONAIDIBUS* pollicetur.   Huc spectant hæ voces
ex tripode sacro, unde oracula certa effari solebant Phœba-
des, ut & versus orationem Phœbi subsequens;
           Annuit & Phœbo jam leni murmure DONA.

44 v. 245   *En! nuncia litera--*FRASERII] An. 1723, mense Sextili,
Honorabilis vir JACOBUS FRASERIUS, literis & virtute insignis, epistolam scripsit ad Academiæ Regiæ Moderatores, in
quâ pollicetur ducentas libras Anglicanas, Bibliothecæ instau-
randæ causâ.   Nec pollicitis defuit fides, pecunia soluta est;
continuò Moderatores Academiæ ædes Bibliothecæ, ædesq;
subjectas, pulcherrimum in modum instaurandas curârunt, u-
ti dictum *Not.* 8.   Quod opus cùm bonâ fide perfectum præsens FRASERIUS ipse noster vidisset & probâsset, mense O-
ctobri, An. (ultimo demum elapso) 1724, alias centum libras
se *Londino* remissurum promittit, ad erigenda *Dunbaria* tecta,
quæ tunc partim solo æquata, partim jamjam casura nutabant.
V. *Not.* 7.   *Londinum* profectus, polliciti sui fidem citò li-
beravit, mense *Novembri* & mense *Februario* ultimò elapsis.
Persolutis his trecentis libris, en! intra paucas hebdomadas
adfertur epistola altera, pollicens alias ducentas libras, ad ulterius provehenda *Dunbaria* tecta.

45 v. 255   ——*esuriens migraret in atria* Clio] h. e. Cùm literarum
Professores ad servilia munera obeunda inopiâ victûs coge-
rentur.   V. *Juv. Sat.* 7. *v.* 4, 5, 6, 7.

46 v. 266

46 *v.266* *Musæ dona libellos, &c.*] Bibliothecam nostram per multos retrò annos libris donare solebat FRASERIUS noster. An.
autem 1723, plurimis ditavit; jam verò pluribus se donatu-
rum pollicetur.

47 *v.271* FRASERIUS—*statuatur*] Statua FRASERII erigatur in mediâ areâ Coll. Regii.

Ovid. Ep. 2. Inter & Ægidas mediâ statuaris in urbe.

48 *v.272* *Atque aliis monstrans*] h. e. Statuatur FRASERIUS eo situ,
ut ingredientibus aream Collegii digito monstrare videatur
tecta, non quæ ipse erigenda curaverit, sed quæ adhuc jaceant imperfecta : quæ quidem vereor ut jaceant, ni Coll. Regio succurrant opes Regiæ.

49 *v.278* —*duplici vittis auroque coronâ*] *Virg. Æn.* —*duplicem gem-
mis auroque coronam.* Hîc autem intellige *Doctoratûs* gra-
dum in utroque jure, & diploma honorem istum conferens,
vittis, variis floribus, aureisque picturis pulcherrimè depi-
ctum, quo nos FRASERIUM nostrum, literis egregium, nuper jure optimo ornavimus. Huc etiam in primis referendus
ultimus Prooemii versus, *Purpureos flores, lilia mista rosis.* Diploma enim *Fraserianum* habet lilia è pixide enata, unà cum
tribus Salmonibus transversis, & manu tenente librum (quæ
Coll. Regii insignia sunt) scitè depicta; ut & rosas rubentes,
aliosque flores, & lauream Coronam virentem, deauratum
nomen *J. F.* cingentem, duasque Cornucopias pomis matu-
ris plenas.

50 *v.293* *Pietate insignis avitâ*] Pietate canâ & priscâ, & quali o-
lim usi fuerant in Academiam Regiam, Cl. *Elphinstonius, Dunbarus, Stuartus,* &c.

51 *v.295* *Munificam mentem*] FRASERIUS, præter munera in Almam nostram Matrem collata, alia in alios plurima & varia
contulit : Fratres duos aut tres, suis impensis, artibus liberalibus instituendos curavit. Liberos suos, duo mares totidemque femellas, ut & ex filio nepotem, egregiis ornavit patri-
moniis. Scoticanam Societatem de propagandâ Christianâ
fide apud Montanos & Insulanos insigni prosecutus est muni-
ficentiâ. Bibliothecam *Innernessensem* libris donavit, ut & quos-
dam V. D. Ministros insulanos, quibus maximè egerent. Flumina quædam pontibus committi jussit, aliaque opera chari-
tatis peregit, dum in Septentrionali *Scotiæ* plagâ commora-
retur ultimo demum elapso anno. Inde jure MUNIFI-
CUM,

CUM, immo MUNIFICENTISSIMUM appelle-
mus FRASERIUM noftrum.

58 v.299   *Usque modum rebus*] *Horat. Sat.* 1, 106.
          Est modus in rebus, sunt certi denique fines,
          Quos ultra citraque nequit consistere rectum.

53 v.304   *Congruus—Naturæ*] *Horat.* 1. *Ep* 10.
          Vivere naturæ si convenienter oportet.

F I N I S.

Mutanda vel Corrigenda.

P. 3. v. 5. *lege*, pietate infignis, in oris His ædes fta-
tuit nobis—— *p.* 7. *v.* 116, *l.* nofque, ut par. *Ibid. v.* 138,
l. ne efuries premeret nos triftis inopfque. *p.* 10. *v.* 218,
l. opprimat. *p.* 11. *v.* 258, *post* deeffe *dele punctum. p.* 12.
v. 294. *l.* pietate infignis avitâ. *p.* 15. *lin.* 16, *l.* inftructum.
p. 17. *not.* 11, *post* cenfemus, *adde*, Nec tamen hoc princi-
pibus viris in inftaurandâ religione, fummâ ufque laude or-
nandis, fed vulgo mobili imputandum arbitramur.

A
POEM,

In Imitation of

DONAIDES,

By DAVID MALLOCH, *A. M.*

IN ancient Times, e're *Wealth* was *Learning's* Foe,
    And dar'd despise the Worth, *he* would not know :
    E're *Ignorance* look'd lofty in a *Peer*,
    And smil'd at Wit, cast back in Fortune's Rear.
The pious * PRELATE, truly good and great,
Courted the *Muses* to this happy Seat.
Friend to instructive Arts, he knew to prize ;
His Bounty bad the mighty Pile arise.

* Bp. El-
ston.

A

Splendor

Splendor adorn'd what knowing *Skill* defign'd;
And the fair Structure fpoke his noble Mind.
The Fabrick finifh'd, to fecure the Fame,
He ftil'd it Royal, from the * Sovereign's Name.

K. James IV.

    Here, by fucceffive *Worthies*, well was taught
All that enlightens, and exalts the Thought.
With Labour planted, and improv'd with Care,
Long, every cherifh'd Science flourifh'd fair.
Thus, without Cloud ferene, the Seafons roll'd ;
Thus, *Learning* faw renew'd the Age of Gold.

    But now, the Years revolving backward ran,
And a dark Series of worfe Time began.
Vile Avarice in * *Gordon's* Time arofe ;
Arts unefteem'd, were govern'd by their Foes.
When *Sacred Structures* fell by *popular Rage,*
Old *Gothick* Piles, not modifh for the Age.
Then fell to low Contempt th' inftructing Trade,
And every *Mufe's Portion* was *unpaid.*

* Bp. *William Gordon.*

    Now, a lone wafte, the *Mufes* Seat appears,
By focial Foes defac'd, and length of Years.
O'er her declining Roofs, with Mofs o'erfpread,
See! *T I M E,* flow-creeping, walks with hoftile Tread,
Silent, and fure, with unremitting Toil,
He fhakes each Wall, and moulders every Pile.
Ruin hangs hovering o'er the deftin'd Place,
And folitary Silence comes apace.

    Learning beheld, with all a Father's Fear,
And mourn'd the total Defolation near !
He faw the *Mufes* ftretch the Wing to fly,
And fpoke his Silent Sorrow in a Sigh !

From

From Heaven in that sad Hour commission'd came
Fair *CHARITY*, in Heaven the foremost Name.
Compassion flew before her, sweetly bright,
And her meek Eyes effulg'd unclouded Light.

" Hear, and rejoyce, the smiling Power begun,
" Full of my Deity, thy * best lov'd *Son* :
" Thy injur'd Rights, regardful, shall assert,
" And nobly take his suffering Parents Part.
" He thy first Favourite, and thy dearest Friend,
" Shall bid thy Walls arise, thy Roofs ascend.
" I see all charm'd, I see the future Frame
" Arising, emulate its ancient Name.
" I see thy long lost Pomp shine out again,
" And every Muse, returning, claim her Reign.
" Nor ends the Bounty here, by him bestow'd,
" *Learning's Rich Stores* shall thy *Musæum* load ::
" What e'er deep hid Philosophy has found,
" Or the *Muse* sung, with living Laurel crown'd ;
" Or *History* descri'd, far-looking Sage !
" In the dark doubtfulness of distant Age :
" These, thy well chosen Treasures, there combin'd,
" Unwasting shall enrich the searchful Mind.
" But teach thy *Sons* the gentle Arts of Peace.
" Let Faction lose his Rule, and Discord cease ;
" Rivals alone in Love, and doing well,
" Be their fair Emulation to excell.
" Then shall encourag'd *Arts*, succesful thrive,
" And all the Glory of the Name revive.

James Brasier Dr. of Laws.

F I N I S.

TEXTUAL NOTES

1.17 *Thus, without Cloud serene, the Seasons roll'd;* corrected in 1743 to "without Cloud, serene the Seasons roll'd;".

1.53 *Nor ends the Bounty here by him bestow'd,* A semi-colon was properly inserted, by hand, after "here" in the copy of the poem at the Beinecke Library. A semi-colon is also found in the version which Robert Anderson printed from the manuscript in *A Complete Edition of the Poets of Great Britain* (London, 1794), ix. 683.

NOTE ON THE TRANSLATION

My Latin is a little lost with my youth, which had a good deal of it. It has, I think, sufficed me here—somewhat to my surprise. Yet I owe, and acknowledge, a debt to Professor Frederick Pottle, the eminent Boswellian, who has explicated certain passages that were obscure to me.

When I came to decide upon the tone of English translation, my worry was that the language I had grown used to in such enterprises, in 1919 (say) to 1926, might put off a contemporary reader. Once upon a time you could tell poetry from prose by the language; now you can tell it only by the mystery.

The Romans were well aware that when they were writing poetry they were not writing prose. Prose was earth-bound, poetry among the stars—a dread tax upon human powers. Virgil could do the thing easily:

> Aspice convexo nutantem pondere mundum
> Terrasque tractusque maris caelumque profundum. . . .

How to translate *that*, with its marvelous itemization of details in the repeated -*que*? "Ordinary language" won't do, because the image is not ordinary, nor is the human experience the image expresses. "Look how the earth shudders within its rounded weight—*and* the lands, *and* the tracts of sea, *and* the deep sky!"

Human speech, the way we talk to one another, is eloquent, especially when unguarded, and is the source of much poetry. But when you want to "rise," given a moment and a theme for rising, you do require, as the eighteenth century believed, a different order of speech. The trouble is, as mere versifiers in the eighteenth century displayed, that the different order of speech will not, of itself, yield poetry.

Accordingly, I have attempted a prose not flat and not stilted, maintaining the exaggeration, the "loftiness," that Ker, with his intimate love of Virgil and Ovid, intended. "Not flat and not stilted"—how else to observe the Augustan golden mean? Ker meant to say that important things are important, and that among these is the destiny of human knowledge. I agree, and I hope I have done service to his wisdom.

Barrows Dunham
Bala-Cynwyd, Pennsylvania

DONAIDES:
or, A Hymn of Thanksgiving from the Aberdonian Muses Concerning the Unexampled Munificence of James Fraser, J. U. D., Toward King's College, Aberdeen.

> Accept, Fraser, generous and famed in your deeds, the little gifts the Children of the Don[1] bring you in thanks: small returns, to be sure, not equal to your splendid gifts, but becoming to us in our poor and humble state. With you, it is silver and abundance of yellow gold: you bless us in the giving and at the same time bless yourself. For our part, we offer the little gifts our garden affords: purple flowers, lilies mingled with roses.

Come then, cheerful and gay, let us sing the Man who restored to us pleasant groves and noble buildings. The Muses' halls, sacred to learning, remained for a long time richly adorned, well made, well furnished: those lasting halls that Elphinstone, noted for piety, raised for us on these shores, establishing thus the seat proclaimed by royal order in the King's name.[2] There, through many ages, the youth were accustomed eagerly to practice the arts, to conduct study with frequent struggle, and to dance in joyful song.

Formerly there was no place more grateful to Apollo nor one in which he took more pride.[3] Leaving the sacred waters, the waves of Permessus, the ridges of Parnassus, he brought us hither to the mouth of the lovely Don, obeying the command itself of highest Jove. Then spoke he thus: "Here we enjoy the choicest site. You see what lofty citadels are Elphinstone's, the high palatial buildings with their exalted columns he has set up for you and has declared to be your own. Hither the Fates call us; into these buildings let us now remove.[4] This is our home; these are our streams and fountains; these, too, our sunny hills and all things green."

Nor was there delay. We hastened with joyful strides, the Father God leading us. We entered the sacred precincts, and with delight we looked up to the new vaulted halls, the Daedalian roofs. Ours then to inhabit the happy mansions and to abide there, settled into placid peace.

And now the Muses leave thy towers, O fair Lutetia; they make haste to the waters of the lovely Don and yearn to dwell there. Hector attends!—our Boece,[5] that most famous leader of the host, and Hay, his comrade and *fidus Achates*. Thus the Muses flourish, and the learned names shine. Thus Gaul repays the ancient gifts of Caledonia, and Charlemagne gives back to Scotus his deserved reward.[6]

After Elphinstone, the sacred fillet of Dunbar and Stewart[7] entwined us, and we accomplished many happy years. The horn of plenty was ever full. Streams flowed now with milk, now with nectar, and yellow honey dripped from the thriving oak.[8] Ceres, the free, the nourishing, gave gladly of her bounty. The forests leaved, the farmers' furrows flourished. Dwellings shone, lamps hung from golden-panelled ceilings, with the assembly applauding joyful dances.

Then came a worse time in the revolving years, with Gordon[9] in control of sacred things. Straightway every kind of wickedness burst into a vein of baser metal.[10] Shame fled, and truth, and faith; and in their stead came fraud and guile, treachery and force, and the cursèd love of possession. For Gordon was no Elphinstone; rather, he foully despoiled all the ancestral revenues and estate—gifts that Elphinstone had consecrated to Minerva. Nevertheless, honor and praise will remain yours, Leslie, despite the time.[11]

Alas (for we who saw the thing must speak), a race not innocent, too little pious when roused by blind zeal, raged in the august citadel and shrine of Athena, whilst it sought to strip the lead from the sacred temple.[12] It would have been a ghastly crime to do such bold deeds, deeds daringly done—a man may temper the account with tears!—except that the highminded Anderson[13] came bravely upon the scene as protector of ourselves and of our holy places. Because of him, our archives, snatched and saved from death, display royal charters and many governmental documents.

Yet that was not the end of our evils. The villains strove to expel from the homeland their own guiltless compatriots. Themis, goddess of justice, suffered exile; Medicine was put to flight. Justinian was ordered to mind his own business, Pope Gregory to put away his rules. Old Hippocrates was stricken, and Galen too.[14] Orpheus, famed for moving the gods or even dire Hell itself with the lyre and strings of song, had no effect on *these* men; and Arion was sent back to the dolphins. Thus Alma Mater, sorrowing, lay with dishevelled hair and shattered limbs; and at her thresholds waited (O horrible!) ill-counselling Famine and loathly Want.[15]

At length the faithful divinities took notice of the wretched Muses. He who by Jove's authority gave laws to the Scots, James VI, generous in works for us, poured out his favors with abundant store, endowing us with further lands and increasing our growth in many ways. Here, Maitland, we will exalt your name above the stars—yours also, Arbuthnot, and yours, noble Stuart.[16]

Thus, in the end, the wicked were not allowed the fruits—greedy Harpies, dread creatures that with hook-like claws tore all the food they stole from us.[17] Meanwhile, the illustrious Patrick Forbes of Corse,[18] a name long established, restored our losses by his own effort, lifted us up again, abject, wretched, in want of everything, and almost spent in all that destruction. In his warm embrace, our weakened Alma Mater grew strong again with much new offspring, and flourished as in youth. He restored also the stolen revenues and the ancestral estates, and compelled the Harpies to vanish in terrified flight. With him as leader,

Themis returned as of old and imposed her laws. Hippocrates himself came back in general rejoicing. Then Orpheus smote his lyre, and Arion sang aloud. Again the age renewed itself in its ancient gold. The Muses wandered through a countryside in flower, and bound their hair with garlands, singing praise.

When Patrick died (alas, how great the grief that then arose!), the College, deprived as of its father, justly mourned. The Church mourned also, grown pale for its lost sire; the realm itself shared the sorrow. Athena silently bowed her head in grief, her eyes suffused with shining tears; and farthest Thule mourned. Father Tweed shrilly wailed for him aloud; the mighty Clyde beat his arms upon the banks resounding with waves; and the Tay, drawn swiftly down from his Grampian height, hurled his waters into violent vortex. The Don sped backward, and with contrary waves flowed into the Grampian Hills. The Dee was borne into the rage and seething of the ocean, and rolled his floods, howling, toward the stars. Ourselves, we made a tomb for Forbes and covered it with various roses, and upon it we set a song.[19]

But the great Forbes was not altogether dead. Truly there are brilliant lights sprung from the golden star that earth, slave to the Little Bear, has marvelled at these many years.[20] O best of fathers, you left a son worthy of yourself, whose name shall thrive through centuries, if there be any honor in piety or grace in doctrine.

Next, Charles I, pitying the needy Muses, willed, with the consent of the Senate, that no profane hand dare carry off the consecrated revenues belonging to the holy fillet of the Don, and thereupon devoted them all to our venerable selves and our Lyceum.[21] (Whence, with great zeal, we caused new wonders to arise: we erected handsome, lofty buildings.) These revenues we gave back when his son was restored to the ancestral throne, but we took little good from that.[22]

After this, we had no help from the higher powers until William of Orange, the hero, looked upon us in our misery—famed cultivator as he was of Athena, of war, and of the toga.[23] Then pious Anna looked on us with joyful light. What Anna bestowed the good George [I] renewed to Alma Mater, lest foul penury should sadly press us down.

There were at that time certain private persons who helped Alma Mater with gifts. To name them all would take too long; but you, Buchanan,[24] must not be left in silence. Let us, in the very courtyard itself, pour out the libation rightfully yours, by whose order our palace was restored.

Here it is likewise fitting to commemorate the men who enriched the Library with books, though we have not the space for doing so. But you, Scougall, and your son[25] must be mentioned—and your names too, Gardner, Fraser, Strachan, Rait, and Stuart. Nor ought we delay to celebrate with equal praise the men who established bursaries. Burnet led this array, and his comrades followed: Watt, Ogilvy, Melvill, Park, Adam, Fullerton, Watson, Margaret Gordon of Braco, and, last of all,

Gregg.[26] These happy souls, pious names, attained the blissful, joyous seats, the glad flowering of pleasant pastures, the places blest.

Nevertheless, our condition was meanwhile not safe. Elphinstone's buildings threatened collapse and miserable decay—ruins horrible to see and wreckage manifold. Ah, again as before, the halls of Dunbar lay stricken. Again the Harpies—dread, foul birds—came of a sudden horribly from the heights, snatched away the banquet, and tore at everything rapaciously. Wherefore all melted away and fell back again into ruin. Again the worthy thresholds waited. Unspeakable!—ill-counselling Famine and loathly Want.

Then we bethought us to send a certain legate to approach the abode of Father Jove[27] (who reigns in the hall of the gods above) and to his courtiers, to report our ineffable hardships. This opinion prevailed: a man was sent who bore requests and as a suppliant voiced them aloud:[28]

"Father on high, help us in our wretchedness, spare thy faithful people, look closely upon us, humbled as we are. Help us now, and may it please thee to help! Consider us, wearied by every kind of difficulty, lacking everything. Leave not neglected the halls sacred to thee of old, nor let the Muses sink into squalid poverty. Drive out the rapacious Harpies!"

There was no delay. Steps were taken. The legate did his duty. Night and day he wearied the Royal Court and all its neighborhood and even Jove himself. That best of fathers, not averse from entreaty, lent an ear, and thereupon gave orders to the guardian Quaestors.[29] The faithful legate pressed and entreated and wearied them with requests and prayers. Alas, the requests in fact failed; they were many and empty for us. Finally, the Quaestors did order an estimate of the cost of rebuilding—nothing more. Higher powers, alas, have little time to attend to small affairs. The mighty waves that labor the mass thrust our small waves aside. No one considered the Muses.

From hence, too, Jupiter had swiftly withdrawn to the coasts of Ethiopia, indeed beyond the farthest reaches of Africa and India. There was no one to preside joyfully over convivial feasts, as once there had been. Yet may he who can quiet the violent floods of the South Seas now command the loud tempests, enchain them, imprison them, and by his mere presence save a fleet that is scattered upon the surface of an entire sea. The fleet sinks by its own tonnage, its heavy cargo of gold: suddenly it goes down, and gives its riches to the deep. Yet perchance he who has shown care for Oxford and Cambridge will show like care for us and for the harbor of the languishing Don.[30]

After this, we passed several years wavering between hope and fear. Toward the end, we lost all hope; we thought that the higher powers, unfavorably disposed, took no heed of us. Saddened with supplication, beating our breasts, turning the while many bitter things in our hearts, we silently went to the portals of the beauteous Don,[31] and there at last we opened our mouths with these words:

"Look upon us, O Don, in our wretchedness. Cover us with thy swift waters, and draw us beneath Nereus' sea. Or thou, Father Phoebus, that seest all things and hast led us hither with thee, lift us on high, bring us again to the waters of sacred Permessus and the ridges of Parnassus, so that gross poverty may not oppress us nor violent ruin seize us, whilst the buildings, their columns lost, collapse in wreckage. All things threaten present death for us. No man appears, such as Elphinstone was, or Dunbar, Stuart, Forbes. Thou knowest these things, Father Phoebus. Lift us on high!"

At once the whole heaven pealed with horrid thunder, and Phoebus' voice was borne to our ears as from the sacred tripod. Sun-splendored, he addressed us with calm voice:

"Your troubles and your hardships have not escaped me, dear Children of the Don. How often I have condoled with your grief! Refresh your spirits and put away mournful fear: perhaps it will be pleasant to remember these things someday.[32] Ye who have endured heavier things, the God will put an end to these also. Steel yourselves, prepare for better times. I led you hither with me, at the command itself of Jove the Father on High. I do not intend you to leave this ancient seat, your own, which the Fates have pledged forever. Even-handed Jupiter will at last (I mistake it not) consider and afford you help: he will delight you with his powers. He will bring it to pass that dire poverty and foul need shall be banished and the rapacious Harpies sullenly take flight. Meanwhile (for Apollo is no vain prophet) an extraordinary protector shall arise, who will renew your privileges and warm you gently at his tender breast."

And the Don gave assent to Phoebus with a soft murmuring.

Exalted by these words, we strode from the river to the buildings. Lo, a letter, already arrived, announced the proffer of many great gifts— a letter signed by Fraser's own hand, which ordered the walls to rise, with rooms of Parian marble for the Muses. The thing was done not once only. Letter after letter came, bringing many mighty gifts.[33]

Come then, cheerful and gay, let us sing the Man and the bountiful gifts that our friend Fraser has heaped upon us. He alone regarded the Muses saddened in that tempest—as when Clio, hungering in the desert valleys of Aganippe, departed into the halls of the gods, and when sons of the Muses thought it neither gross nor disgraceful to become, as it were, public criers who on funeral occasions call people together at the crematory ovens,[34] and when, alas, Jupiter has no leisure to attend to our straitened affairs, and when, alas, no Maecenas protects the Muses nor any son cares for Alma Mater. Fraser alone looked upon her with joyful light. He raised the fallen courts of the Muses, the ruined halls. He built them high upon lofty columns, with marvelous skill of execution. He ordered everything to be made bright with pure marble, to glisten with large windows. He brought innumerable books as gifts to the Musaeum. He gives, he has given, he will give again. Therefore let the halls of Elphinstone and Dunbar sound forth Fraser. Let his name and arms be preserved, cut upon marble. Let Apelles paint him. Let his statue be set in the very midst of the buildings, and, pointing not to what he has built but to what still lies fallen, let him leave to others the rebuilding of it.[35]

Lo, the Nymphs bear thee baskets of white lilies, roses softly red and mixed with violets. They pluck myrtle, ivy, and crowns of laurel; then of these varied leaves they weave garlands, and bind thy head round with twofold fillets[36] and a crown of gold.

Kind Fraser, chief care of the Muses, it is not in our power to offer sufficient thanks. The gods will grant you rewards worthy of your great merit—Nestorian years, all happy things and fortunate. Pure virtue and a mind conscious of its rectitude are well-pleasing. You have embraced virtue in its sole self; you care nothing for rewards. What joyful ages have brought you forth! How many parents will bow down to such a man! While rivers shall flow to the sea, and shadows arch across the mountains, and the sky pasture the stars, ever your name and praise and honor shall abide.[37]

Come then, cheerful and gay, let us raise to the stars the Man to whom God granted a bosom imbued with generous sincerity, whom ardent virtue has lifted to the skies. Kind Fraser, famous for ancestral piety, the gods have bestowed on you riches and a munificent mind.[38] These you have wisely given over to their proper uses. The miser may learn from you how to employ his wealth—he that delights in little money-chests, and rejoices in heaped-up gold. Most noble Fraser, generous and renowned in deeds, you that know how to put moderation in things and strict limits upon them, that also know how to dwell in harmony with kindly Nature: Live, thrive happily, and may all things issue prosperously for you!

Many of these are drawn from the Latin notes appended to the poem—notes doubtless also written by Ker, no other source being indicated. When a note has its source in Ker, we have marked it JK. We have corrected the notes where necessary, and have added some of our own. The spelling of the names conforms with George F. Black, *The Surnames of Scotland* (New York: New York Public Library, 1946) and Mrs. Margaret Stuart, *Scottish Family History* (Edinburgh: Oliver & Boyd, 1930).

Barrows Dunham

Irma S. Lustig

1. *"Donaides"* is here translated "Children of the Don." Professor Frederick Pottle suggests "Daughters of the Don" in the first instance, a translation that makes the *Donaides* synonymous with the *Musae Aberdonenses*. In 1. 288 Apollo addresses his supplicants as *Donaides carae*, and the feminine ending of the adjective does indeed suggest "Daughters of the Don." In 11. 210-211, however, the verbs *ibamus* and *resolvimus* ("we went . . . to the Don" and "we opened our mouths") are emphatically first person plural. Indeed, the "we" is everywhere present throughout the poem, and refers to all the scholars, past and present, connected with King's College, Aberdeen. The Greek patronymic suffix of *Donaides* is of common gender, and the lovely ambiguity that Latin allows and even promotes will also let the name represent Muses, daughters, and offspring in general, as Professor Pottle agrees.

2. James IV, at the urging of William Elphinstone, Bishop of Aberdeen and first Chancellor of the College. A papal bull sanctioning the University (to be modelled after the Universities of Paris and Bologna) was issued 10 February 1494-95. The Bishop of the diocese was always to be Chancellor.

3. A paraphrase of Virgil, *Eclogue* VI. 73: ". . . *se plus jactet Apollo."*

4. Elphinstone's first buildings at King's College (originally the College of St. Mary), its chapel and crowned tower, residence and classrooms, were erected largely out of savings from his episcopal revenues, and were completed in the autumn of 1505. He also, says JK, began the building of separate houses, with yards and gardens, for the professors of Canon Law, Civil Law, Medicine, and Grammar, but died before finishing them. Dunbar completed the work.

5. Hector Boece, the first Principal of the College, whom Elphinstone summoned from the University of Paris (Lutetia), where he too had been student and lecturer. Boece's book, *The Lives of the Bishops of Aberdeen*, though a mixture of fact and fable, is the major source of information about Elphinstone. William Hay, the first Subprincipal, succeeded Boece.

6. John the Scot (John Scotus Erigena, as he is redundantly known) was a leading intellectual at Charlemagne's court. The return of Boece and Hay from Paris to Aberdeen constitutes the manner in which "Gaul repays the ancient gifts of Caledonia."

7. Gavin Dunbar (d. 1532) did much building for the University, and maintained the departments of Canon Law, Civil Law, Medicine, and Grammar. William Stewart, Bishop of Aberdeen and Chancellor of the University, succeeded Dunbar. He enlarged the buildings on the east and north (JK).

8. Ker here shows a filial respect for the Roman notion that honey was produced by the oak trees it appeared on. See Virgil, *Eclogue* IV. 30: *"et durae quercus sudabunt roscida mella."*

9. William Gordon, appointed in 1546, who began rather well, but soon after, "either sunk in the filth of appetite, as is commonly said, or led on by hate of the established religion," so plundered the property of the Church at Aberdeen as to leave "what scarcely would suffice a Genevan Presbyterian" (JK).

10. The Iron Age. This sentence is a direct quotation from Ovid, *Metamorphoses*, I. 128–129. We owe this identification, which we gratefully acknowledge, to John I. McEnerny, Professor of Classical Languages, Villanova University.

11. John Leslie, "eloquent writer on Scottish affairs, well-known for his loyalty to Queen Mary" (JK). He was Professor of Canon Law in King's College, and, afterward, Bishop of Ross. He died an exile in Brussels, 1596.

12. A mob from the Mearns had pillaged the Cathedral Church and carried away its leaden roof, and set out to do the same with the College buildings. They were prevented by Principal Anderson (JK). Ker observes, the capitals being his own, "We give entire praise to the defenders of a purer religion and to the zeal for establishing it—but zeal for tearing down buildings sacred to the HIGHEST DIVINITY or to the Muses we judge to be scarcely laudable."
    The Privy Council of Scotland actually ordered the roofs of Aberdeen and Elgin cathedrals to be stripped and sold, and the lead was shipped to Holland, as Dr. Johnson reported after seeing the ruins of the cathedrals. The apparent indifference to human life in his comment, "I hope every reader will rejoice that this cargo of sacrilege was lost at sea," brought down on Johnson the outraged ironies of Horace Walpole and Edward Gibbon, among others. (*A Journey to the Western Islands of Scotland*, ed. Mary Lascelles [New Haven and London: Yale Univ. Press, 1971], pp. 23-24, n. 3 and 4.)

13. Alexander Anderson, last Principal of the College before "the restoration of religion." He was deprived of his office for adhering to Catholicism.

14. The references are to Justinian's *Corpus Juris Civilis* and the *Regulae Pastoralis Liber* of Pope Gregory I. Hippocrates and Galen were, of course, celebrated physicians of ancient Greece.

15. This is Virgil, *Aeneid*, VI. 276, in Fairclough's translation. Ker repeats the phrase in 1. 167. Arion was a legendary poet of the 7th century B.C. who was said to have been saved, on one occasion, by the intervention of dolphins. All this symbolism conveys the fact that the departments of Canon Law, Civil Law, Medicine, and Grammar were for a time abandoned. For some years there was a factional struggle over this measure in the *Nova Fundatio*, a plan for reorganizing the University of Aberdeen in the style proposed for the three Scots universities by Andrew Melvill, a great Reformation educator. His program was adopted at Glasgow, where he was Principal, in 1577. It was also adopted at St. Andrews.

16. Robert Maitland, Dean of Aberdeen and a Senator of the College of Justice; Alexander Arbuthnot and Walter Stuart, "most excellent Principals of King's College" (JK). Though Arbuthnot, first to hold office under the Reformation, was anti-episcopal in the Church and adopted some of the methods of his friend Melvill, he was praised by the opposition for his learning, godliness, and good temper. It was after the accession in 1583 of Stuart, an adherent to the Melvill-Arbuthnot party, that the General Assembly approved the

Nova Fundatio for Aberdeen. The change, however, was forbidden by the King.

17. According to JK's note, the "harpies" were men who, by maneuverings more or less legal, seized the houses, gardens, and lands of professors in all four departments.

18. Patrick Forbes of Corse, Bishop of Aberdeen, who became Chancellor in 1619. He has been called the second founder of the University, because, under his administration, the exiled professors returned, and there was much building and rebuilding.

19. When Patrick Forbes died, the various eulogies in prose and verse, in *"elegantissima Latina & Vernacula,"* were collected into a quarto volume edited by his son and entitled *Tomb of the Most Reverend Father Patrick Forbes, Bishop of Aberdeen* (JK). The song, the *carmen*, is six Latin verses by Arthur Johnston. They applaud "an incomparable father and son, each a star of his age," and they lament the son's too early demise. Patrick Forbes had appointed his son John, at the age of twenty-six, to be the first Professor of Theology.

20. Some of the "brilliant lights" were William Leslie, Principal of King's College; Alexander Scrogie, a regent; Alexander Ross, Rector; Robert Baron and James Sibbald, Professors in Marischal College (founded 1593). Other names follow in Ker's notes. The men above, known, with John Forbes, as the six "Aberdeen doctors," were celebrated for having signed the thirteen *General Demands Concerning the Late Covenant Propounded by the Ministers and Professors of Divinity in Aberdeen* (July 1638) and the *Duplyes* (printed in September). Leslie, Scrogie, and Sibbald were deposed by a Commission of Assembly in 1639, after Montrose and his army forcibly converted Aberdeen to Covenanting principles. Two years later, John Forbes was deposed for refusing to subscribe the Covenant.

21. JK's note is, "The succession of bishops among the Scots having been terminated in 1641, Charles I devoted to the University of Aberdeen the entire revenues of the Cathedral. Of these, King's College received two-thirds, Marischal College one-third."

22. JK's note is, "In 1661, when Charles II was restored, the Bishop of Aberdeen got his revenues back, and a donation to King's College was made from the revenues of the churches in the diocese of Aberdeen, Moray, and others, which happened to be vacant. But we had little income from that arrangement."

23. That is, William III, skilled in wisdom, war, and politics, who allotted the University three hundred pounds sterling annually from the revenues of the Scots bishoprics (JK). Ker's epithets emphasize the acceptance of the settlement of 1688 and of the Hanoverian succession.

24. John Buchanan, who in 1707 extended the southern flank of the College (JK).

25. Patrick Scougall and his son Henry, Professor of Sacred Theology, who died at the age of 28.

26. The list begins with scholars and ends with a merchant.

27. "Father Jove" is George I and he only. "Jove" in this allegory is the reigning monarch. Other sovereigns of Scotland and Great Britain have been mentioned, but they are now superseded deities, like Saturn or Uranus. (We owe this insight, and indeed the words themselves, to Professor Pottle.)

28. George Chalmers, Principal, who in 1718 went to the court of George I in search of aid.

29. In Roman times, the Quaestors were officials who dealt ordinarily with the government's financial affairs.

30. George I again, who had given aid to Oxford and Cambridge.

31. An allusion, Ker's note points out, to *Iliad* I. 34: "And he went silently along the shores of the loud-roaring sea."

32. A direct quotation of Virgil's well-known lines, *Aeneid* I. 202–203.

33. In August, 1723, Fraser gave two hundred pounds for restoration of the Library; in October 1724, one hundred pounds more; then, later, another two hundred pounds. He also donated some three hundred books (JK).

34. *A Companion to Latin Studies* (Cambridge University Press, 1921) says (§ 227) that to the funeral of an important person "the people were invited by a public crier (*praeco*)." The plural, *praecones*, is Ker's word here, and he adds the fact that Roman funerals customarily ended in cremation of the corpse.

35. There was an Ovidian precedent for this injunction, *Heroides* 2. 67: "In the midst of your city, even among the sons of Aegeus, let your statue be erected." With Ker, George I's parsimony is reproached by the statue's pointing to the unrestored buildings. Fraser's portrait, done at his own expense, hangs at King's College, and his armorial bearings are on the south wall of the Chapel.

36. The "twofold fillet" signifies the doctorate in both kinds of law, Canon and Civil.

37. A direct quotation from Virgil, *Aeneid* I. 607–609.

38. Fraser, a considerable philanthropist, made other donations: to the Inverness Library and to the Scottish Society for the Propagation of the Christian Faith among the Peoples of the Mountains and Islands. Wherefore, in his notes and with capitals, Ker affirms that Fraser ought to be called, not merely MUNIFICUM (the poem refers to his *mentem munificam*), but MUNIFICEN-TISSIMUM.

WILLIAM ANDREWS CLARK
MEMORIAL LIBRARY
UNIVERSITY OF CALIFORNIA, LOS ANGELES

The Augustan Reprint Society
PUBLICATIONS IN PRINT

The Augustan Reprint Society

PUBLICATIONS IN PRINT

Publications of the first eighteen years of the society (numbers 1 - 108) ar available in paperbound units of six issues at $16.00 per unit from Krau Reprint Company, Route 100, Millwood, New York 10546.

Publications in print are available at the regular membership rate of $5.0 for individuals and $8.00 for institutions per year. Prices of single issue may be obtained upon request. Subsequent publications may be checked i the annual prospectus.

Make check or money order payable to

THE RE⬛⬛⬛⬛⬛⬛⬛⬛⬛ CALIFORNIA

The Wi⬛⬛⬛⬛⬛⬛⬛⬛⬛⬛⬛⬛al Library
2520 Cima⬛⬛⬛⬛ ⬛⬛⬛⬛⬛⬛⬛⬛ ⬛alifornia 90018